The Earth is a very small stage in a vast cosmic arena.
—Carl Sagan

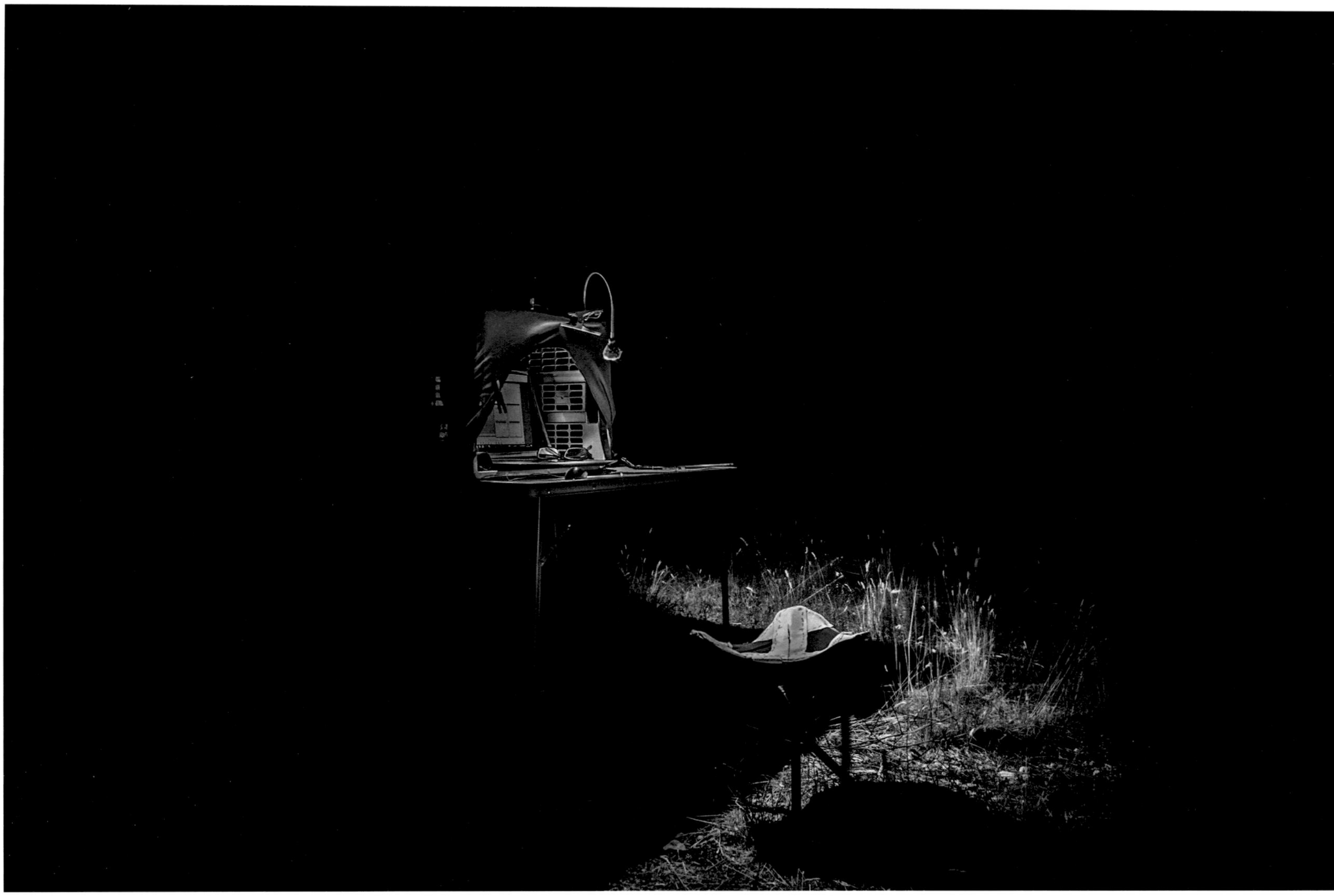

DANIEL STEPHEN HOMER

ROUTE DE LA BELLE ETOILE

GOST

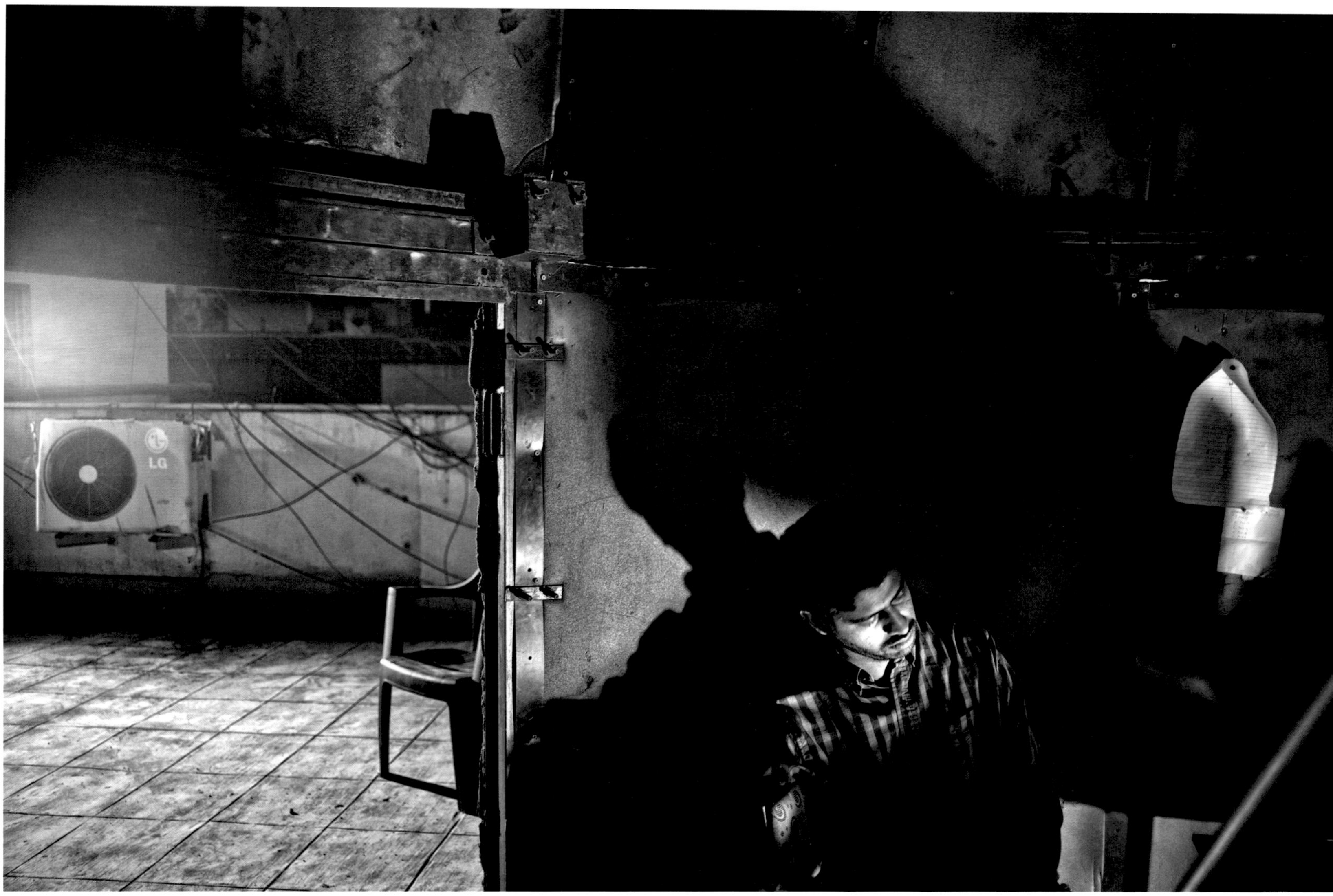
LG

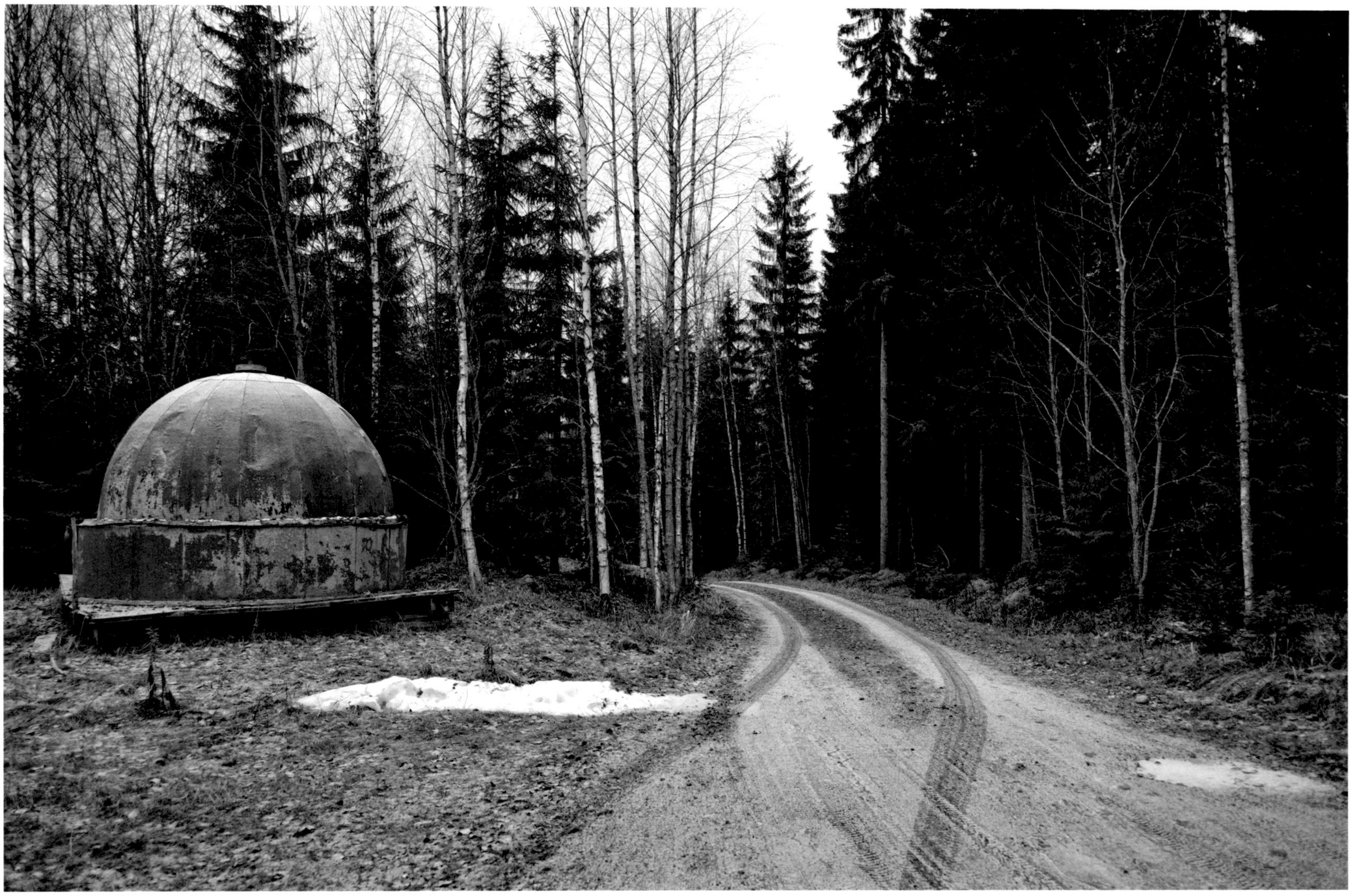

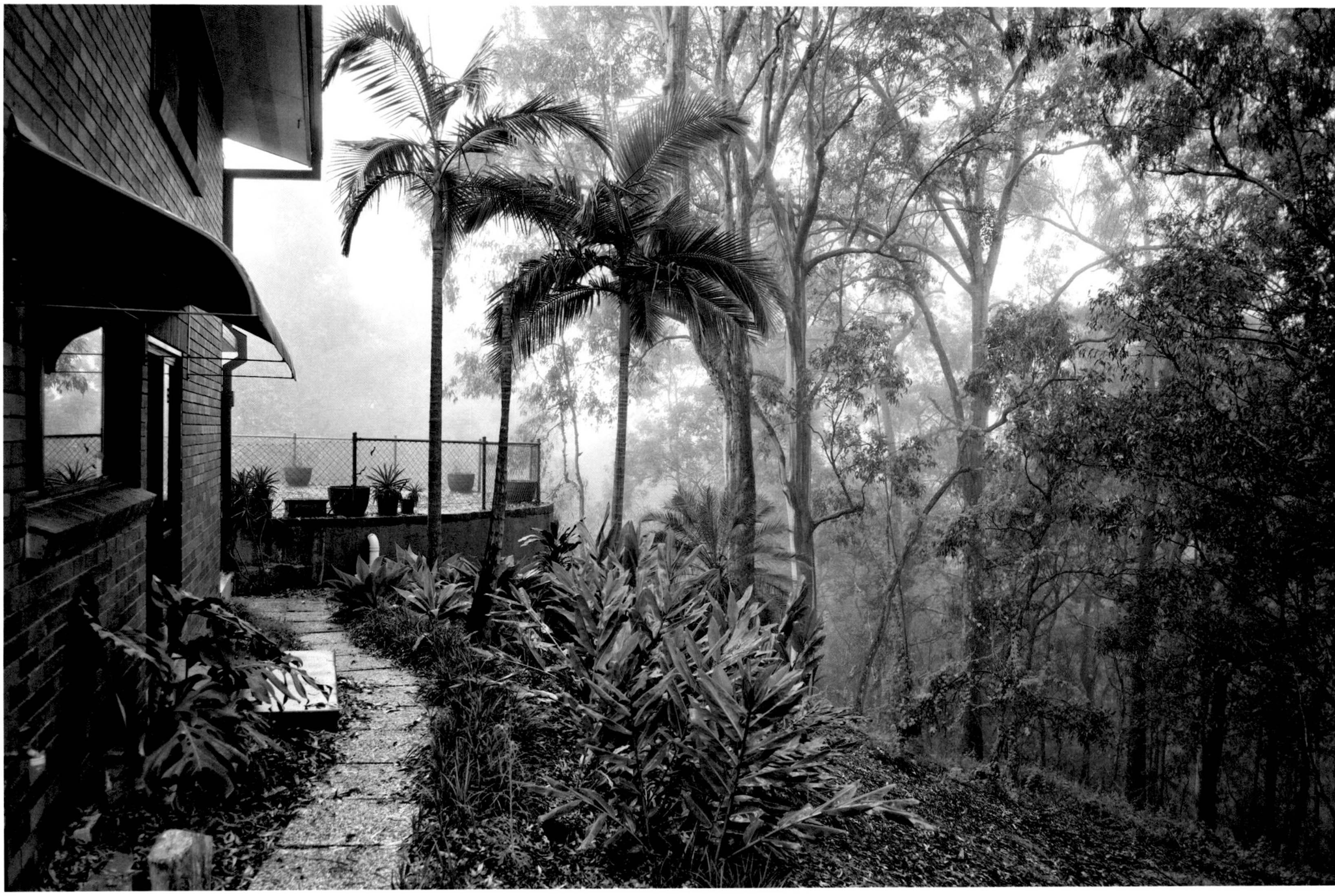

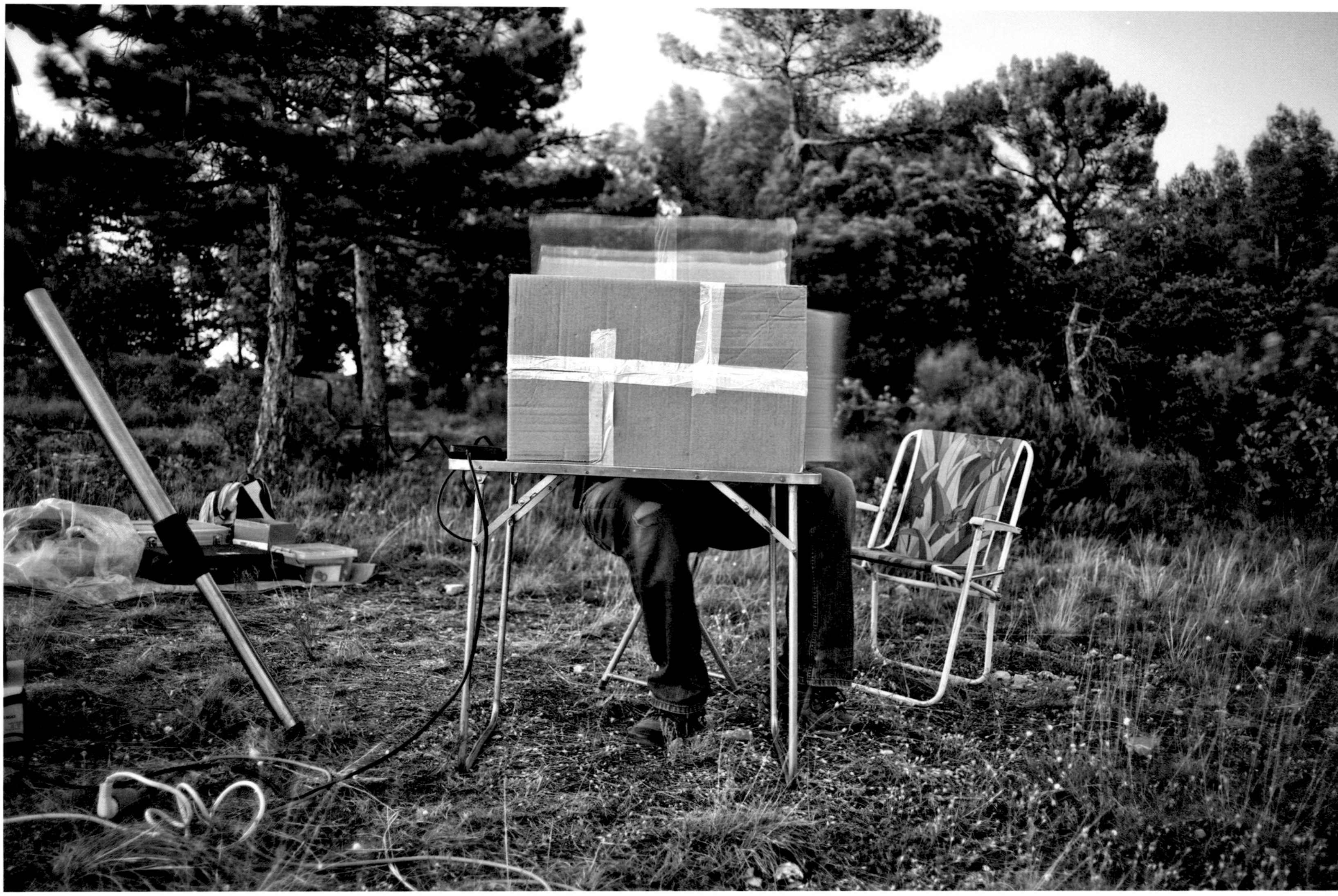

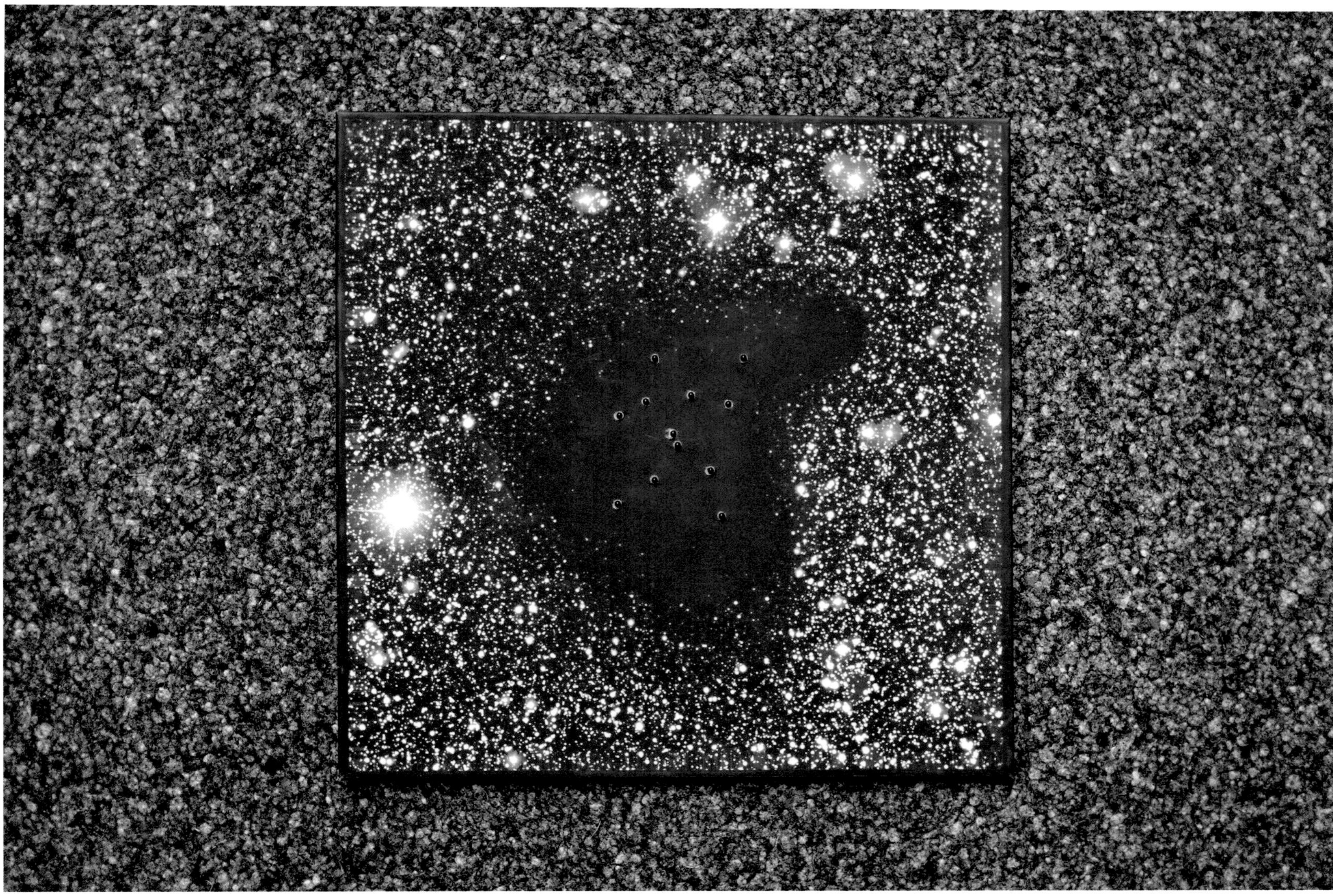

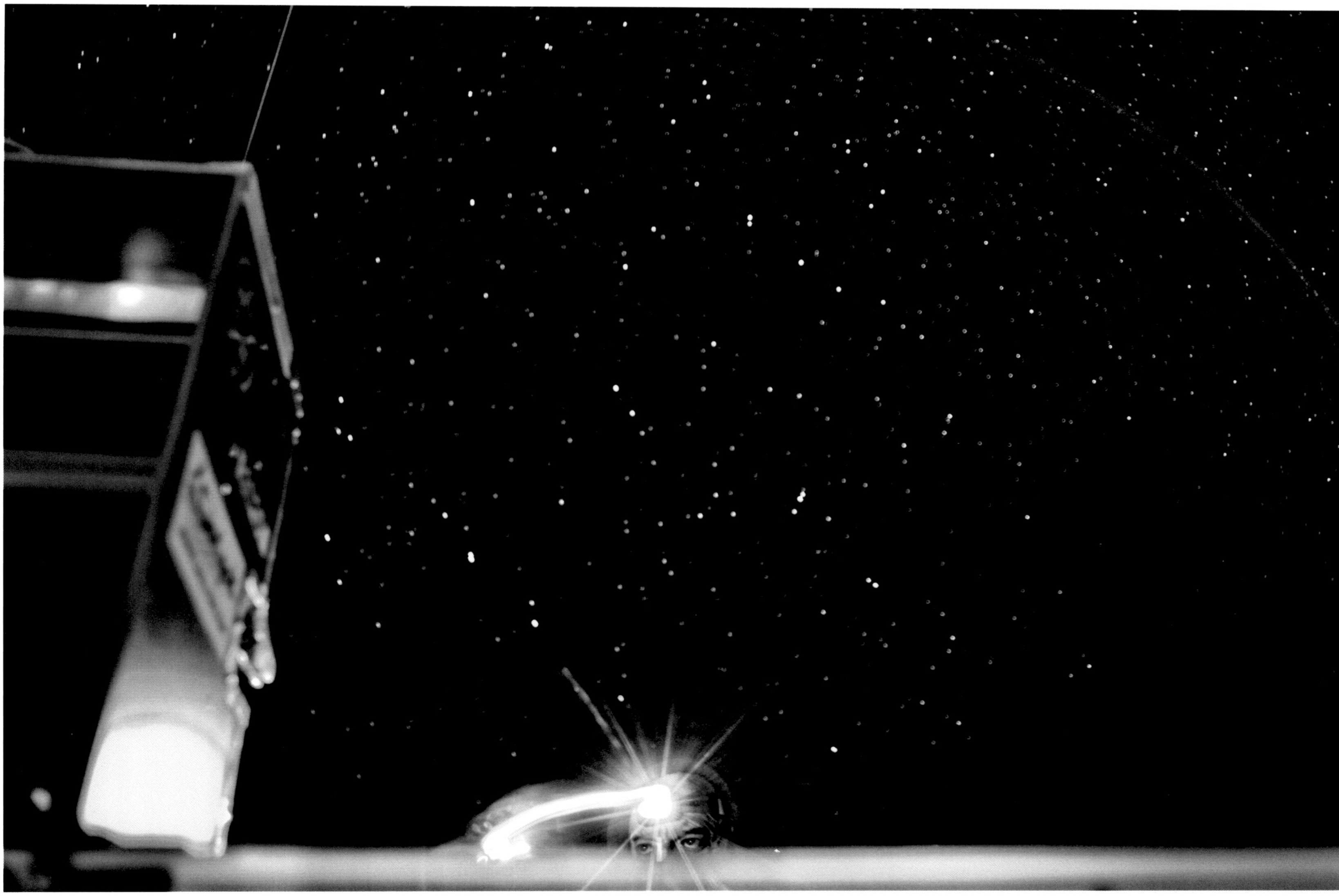

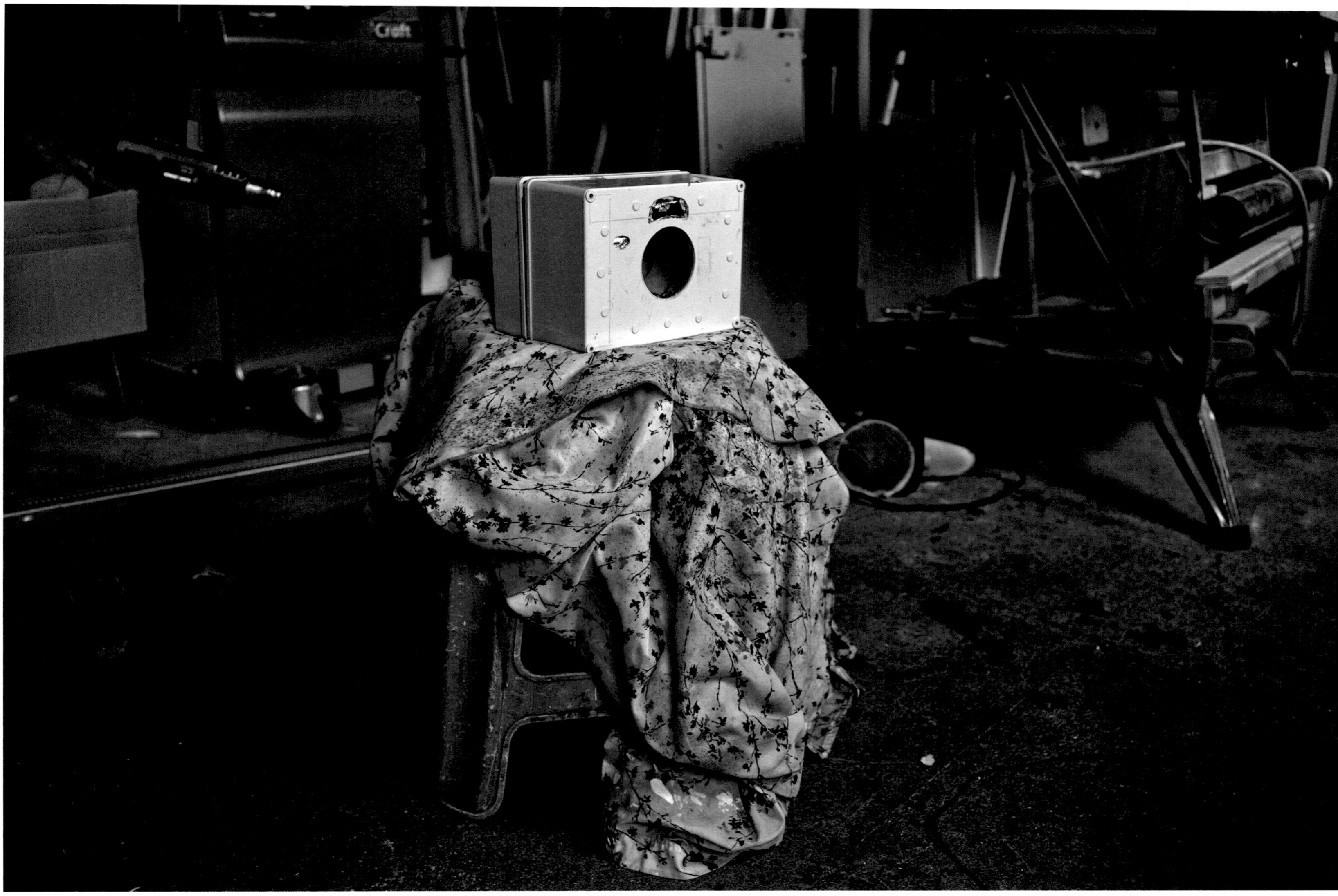

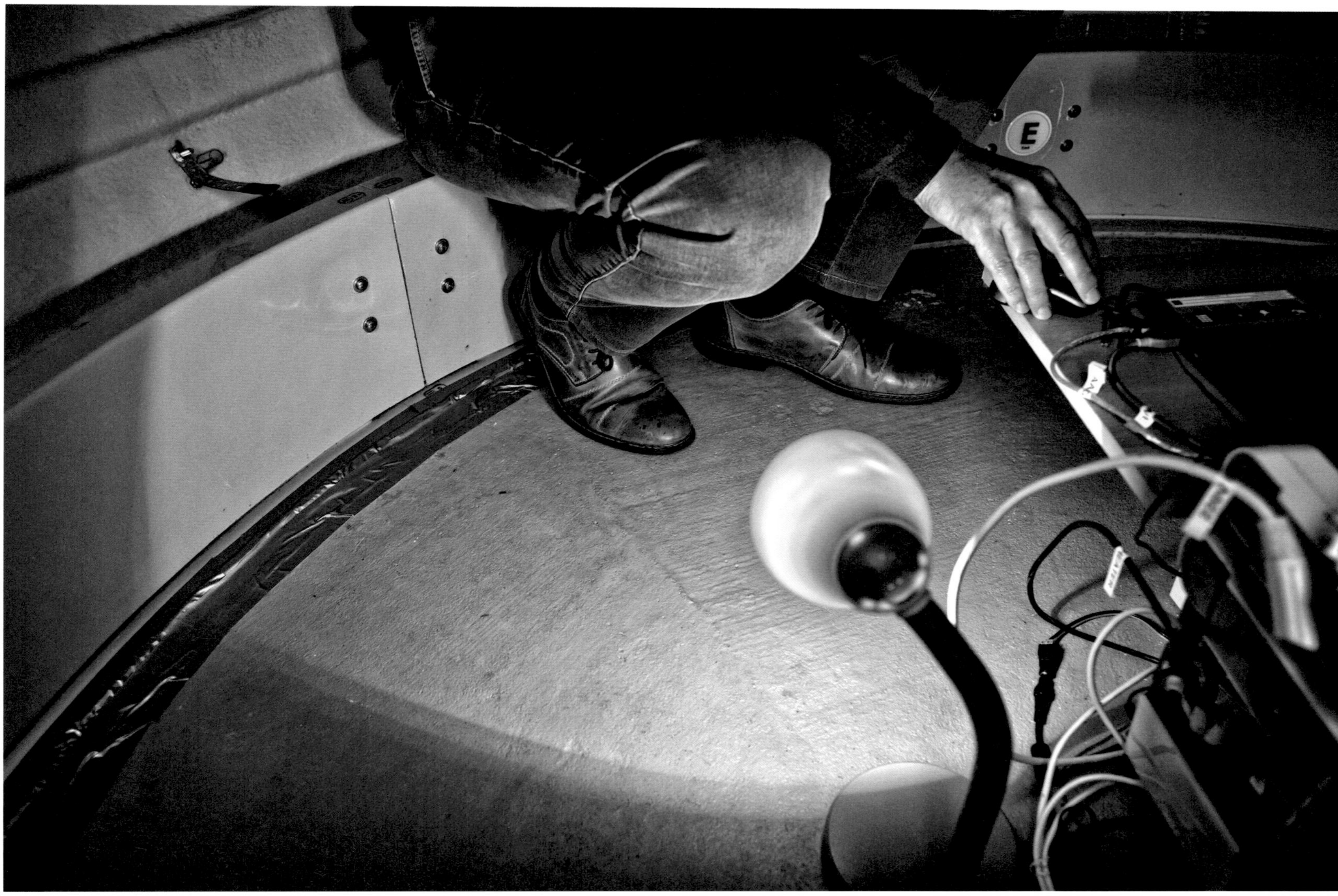

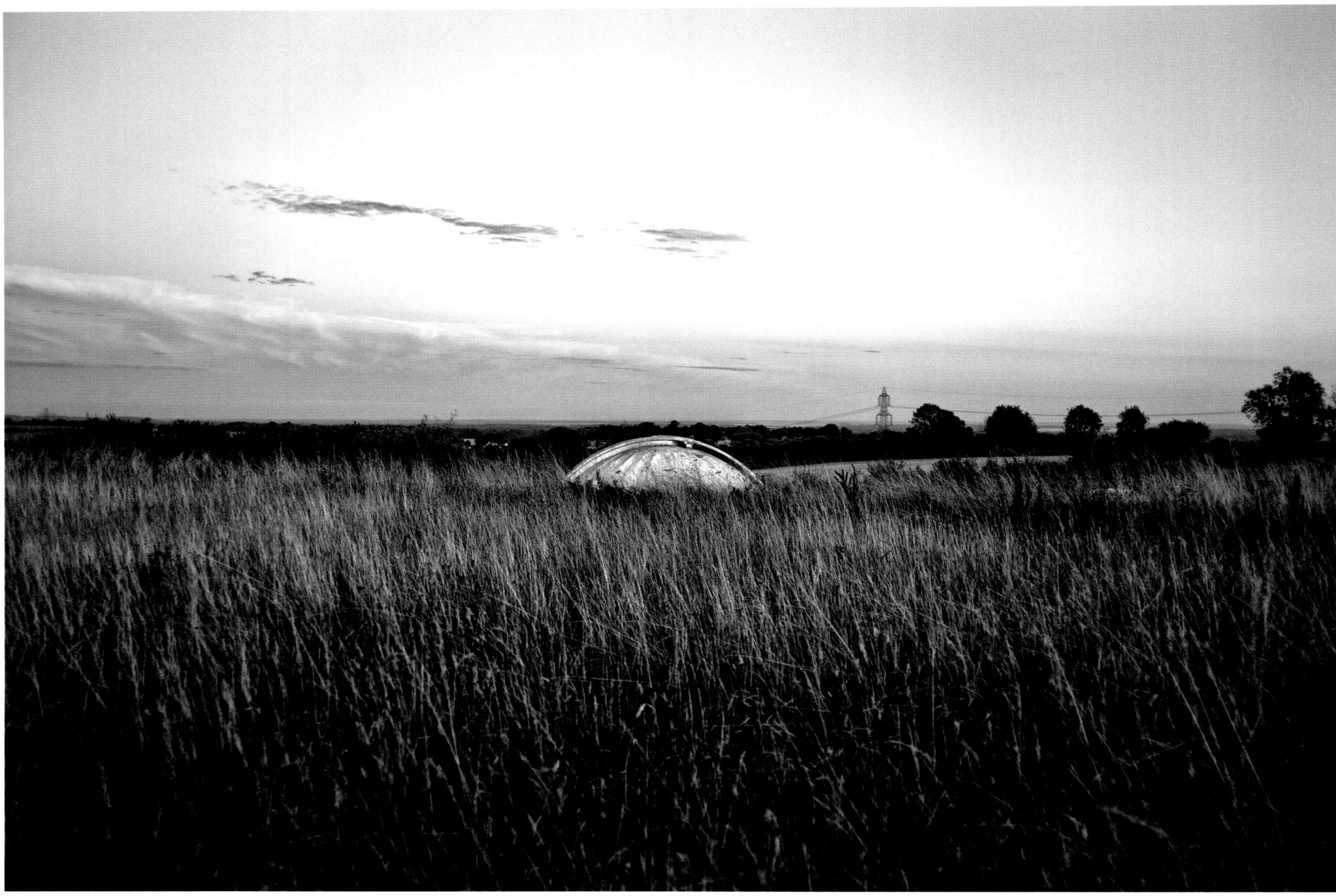

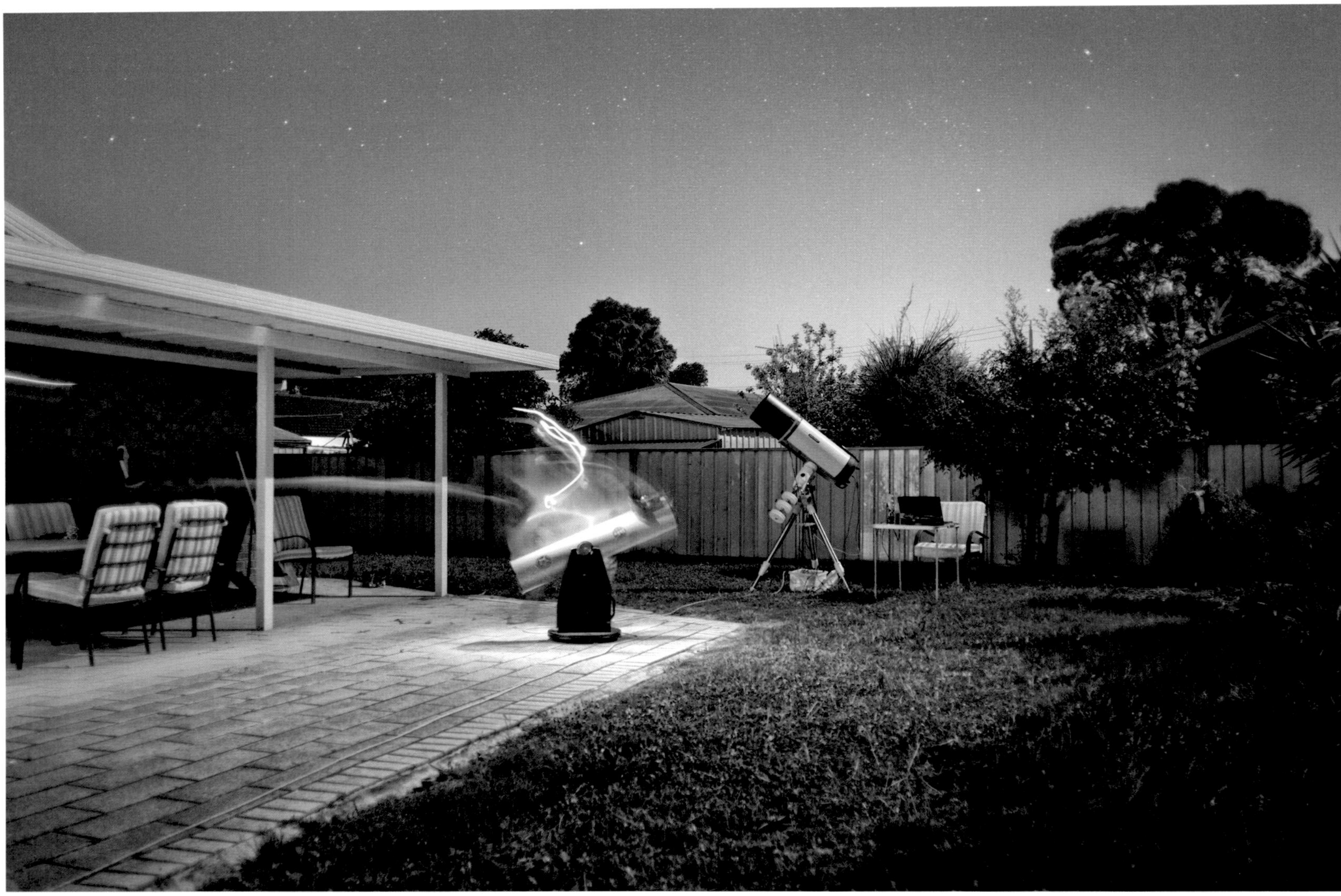

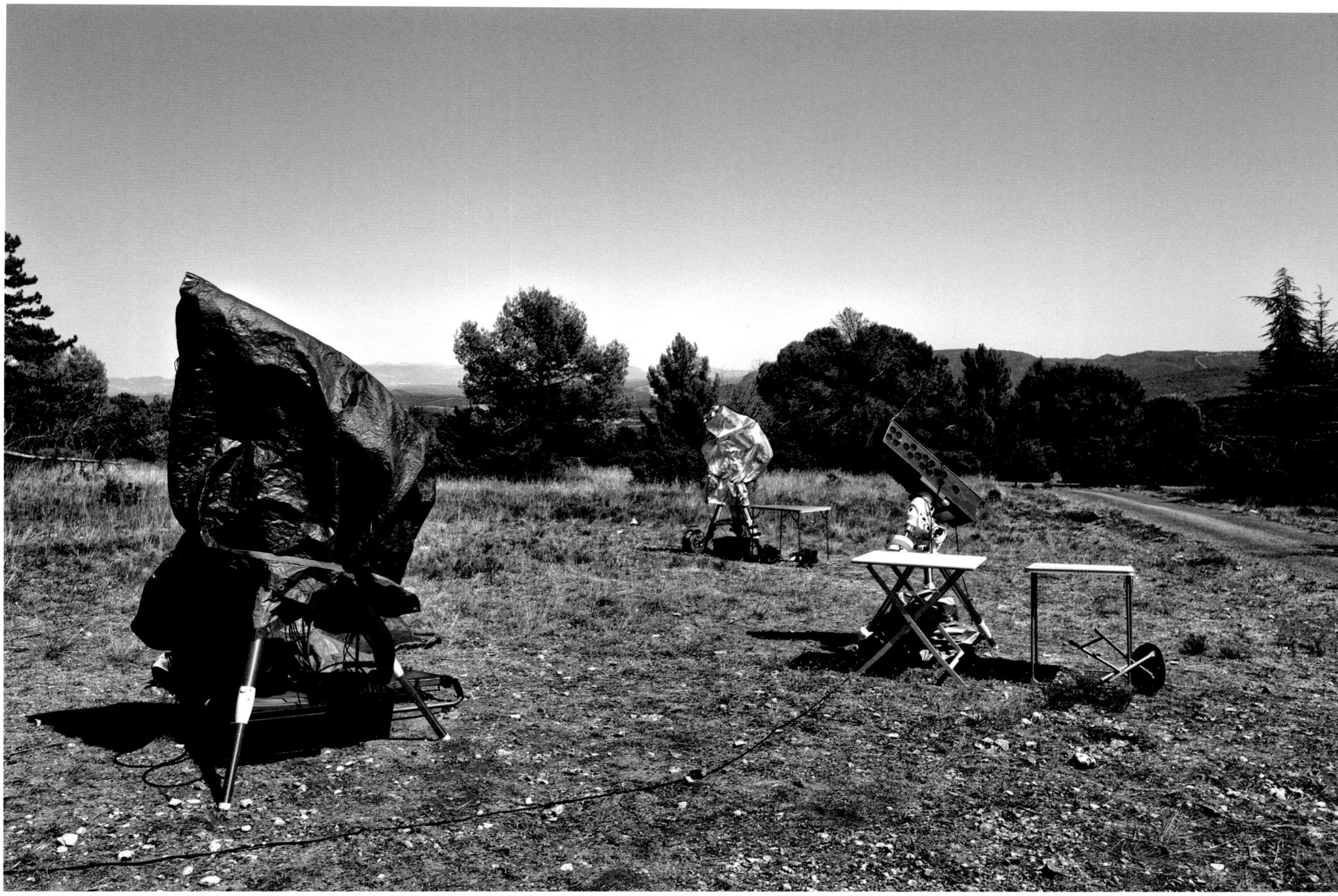

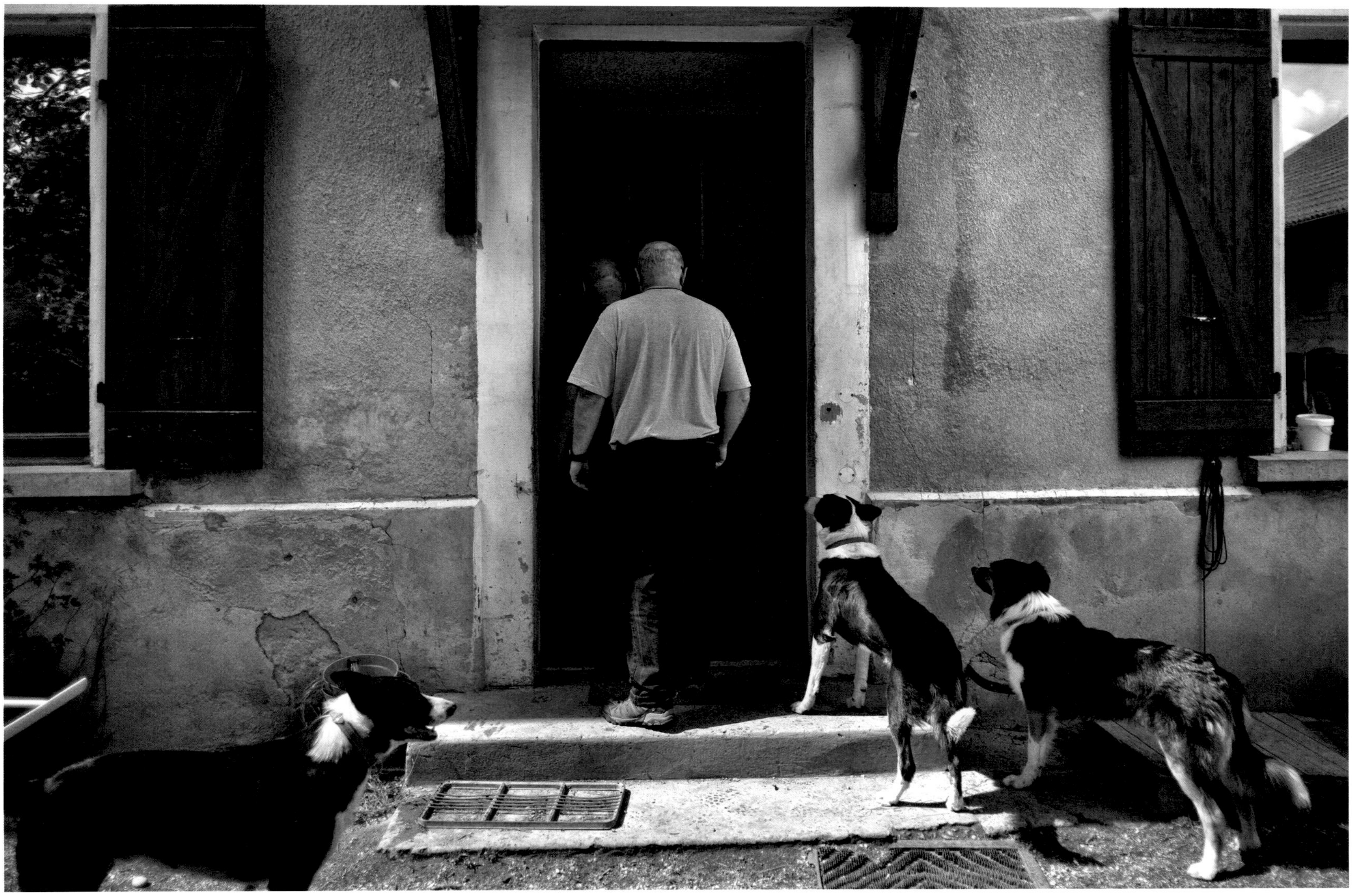

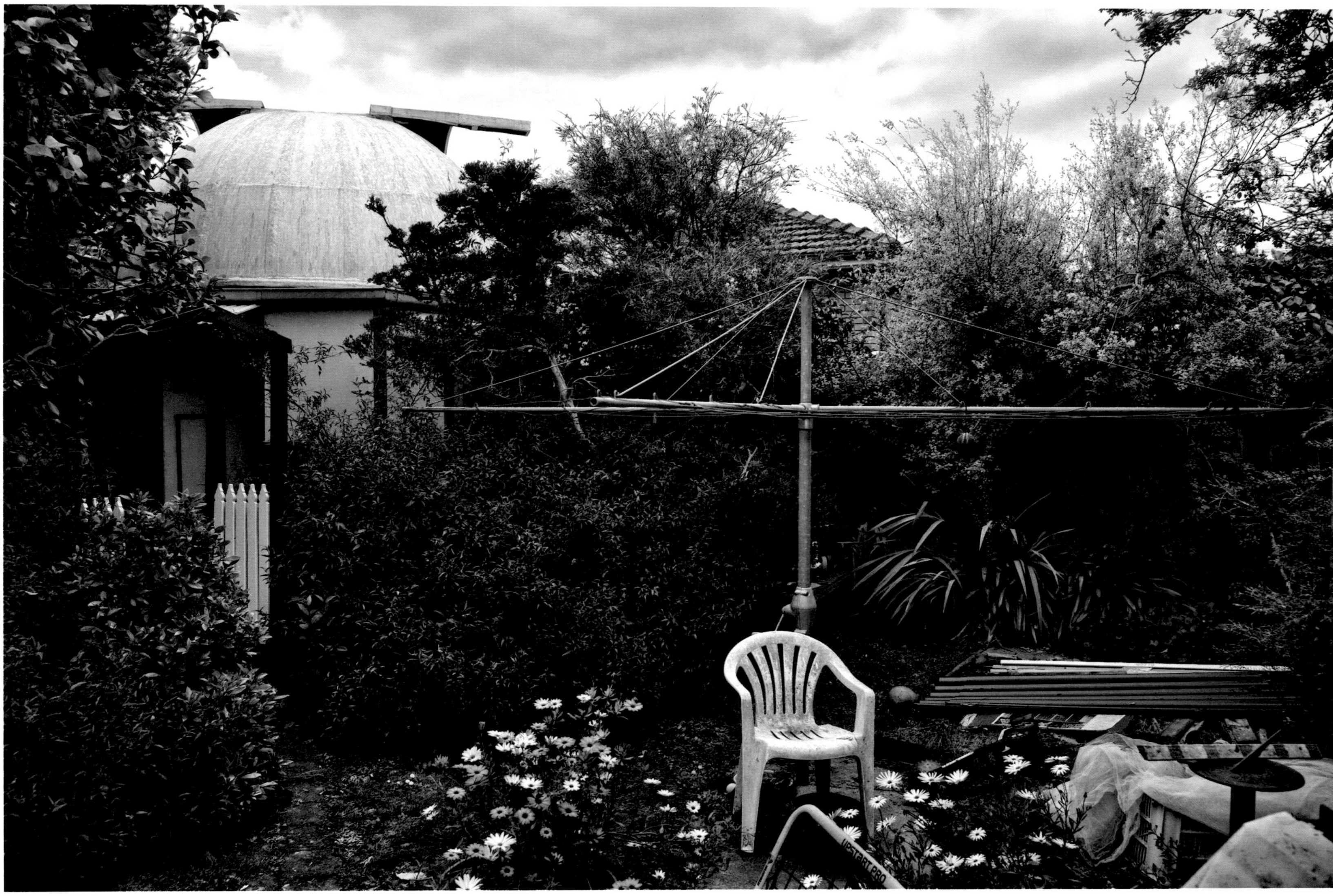

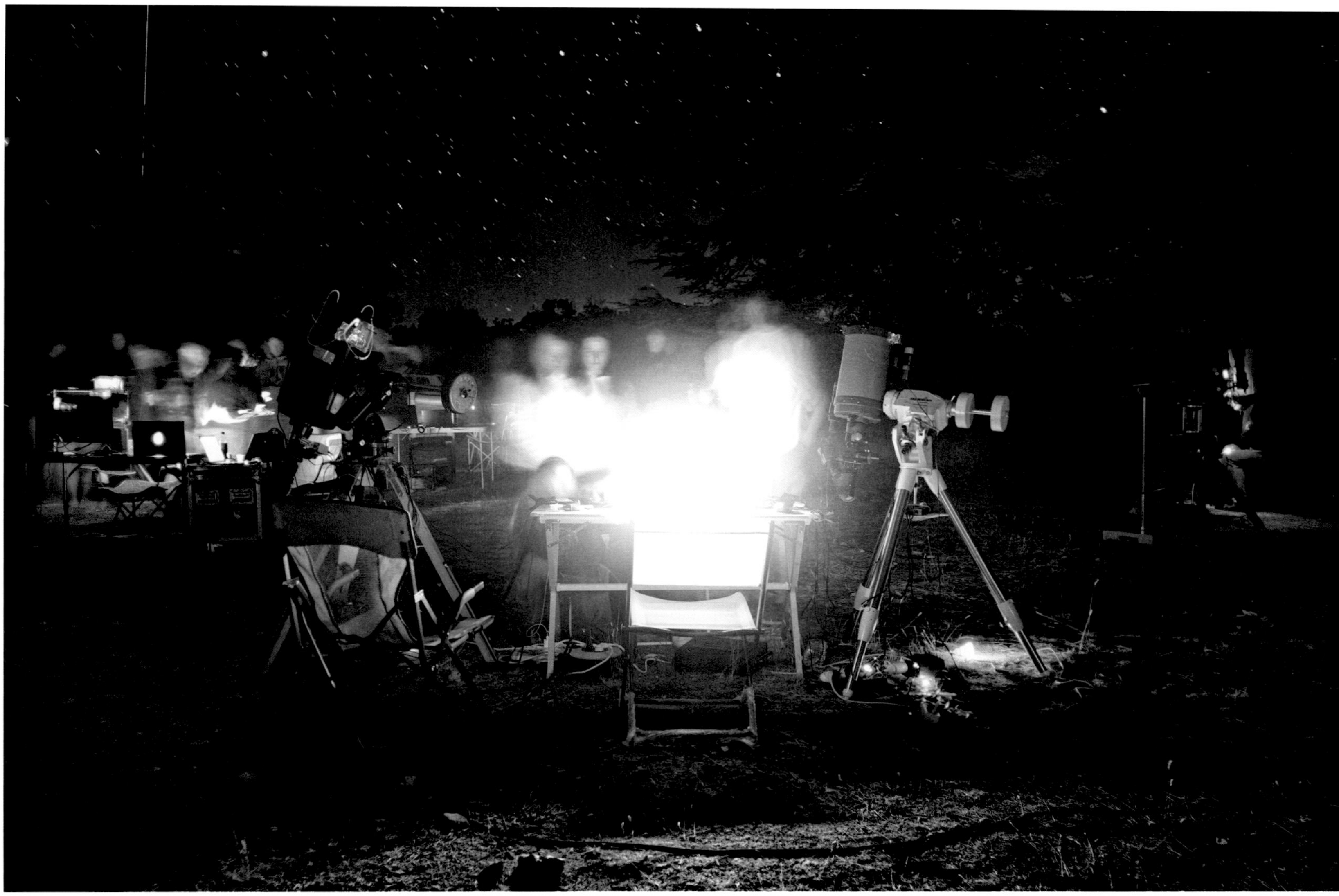

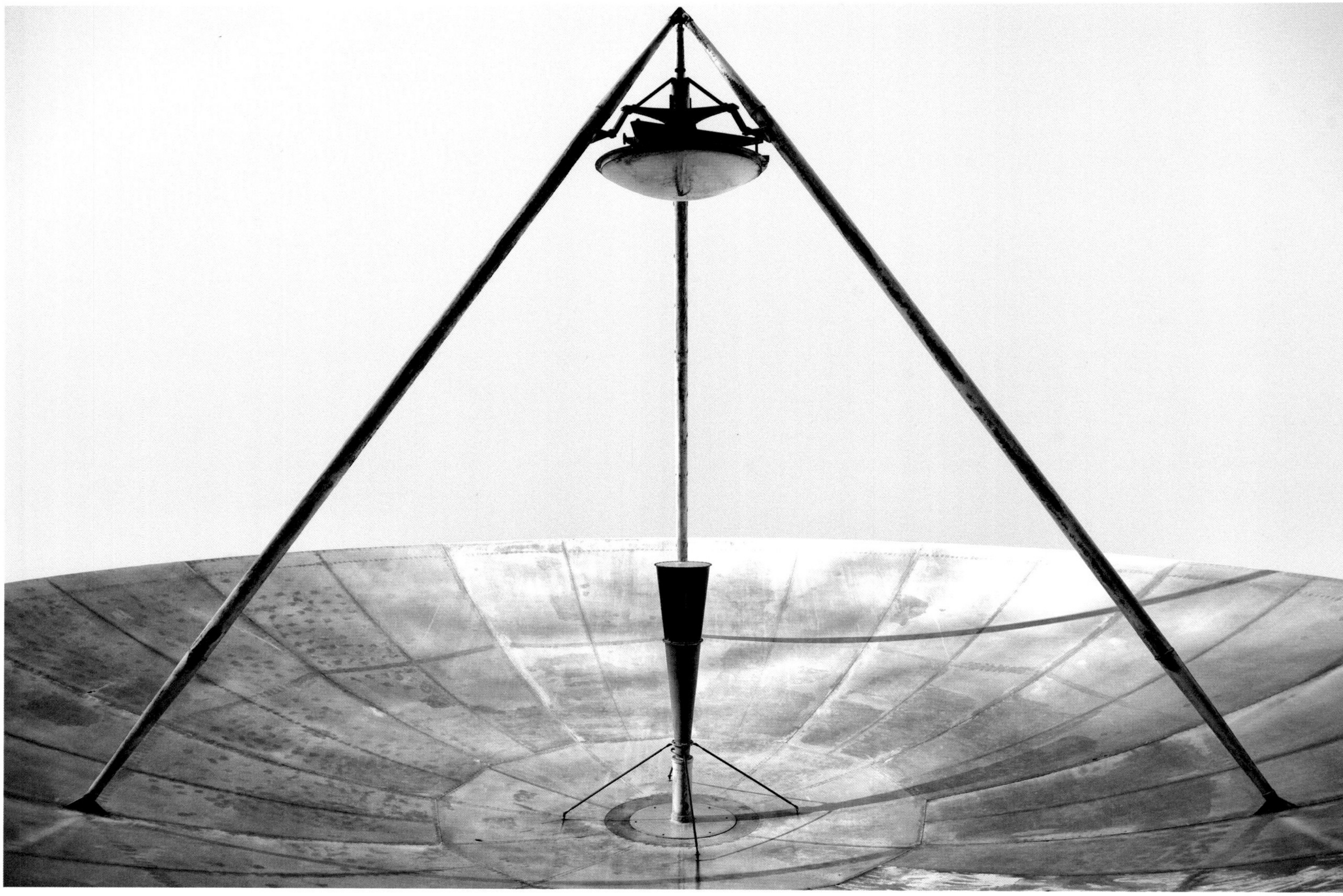

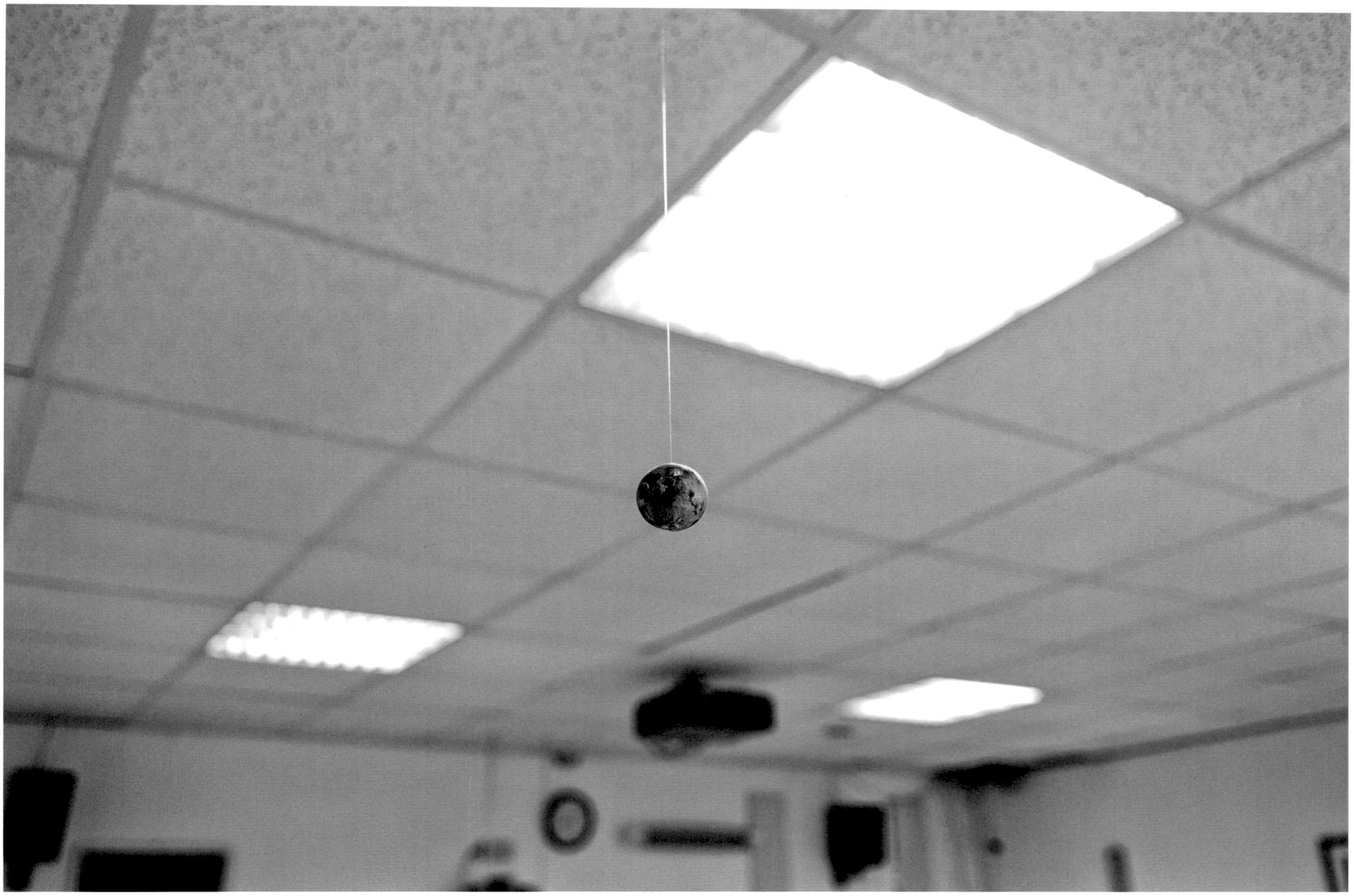

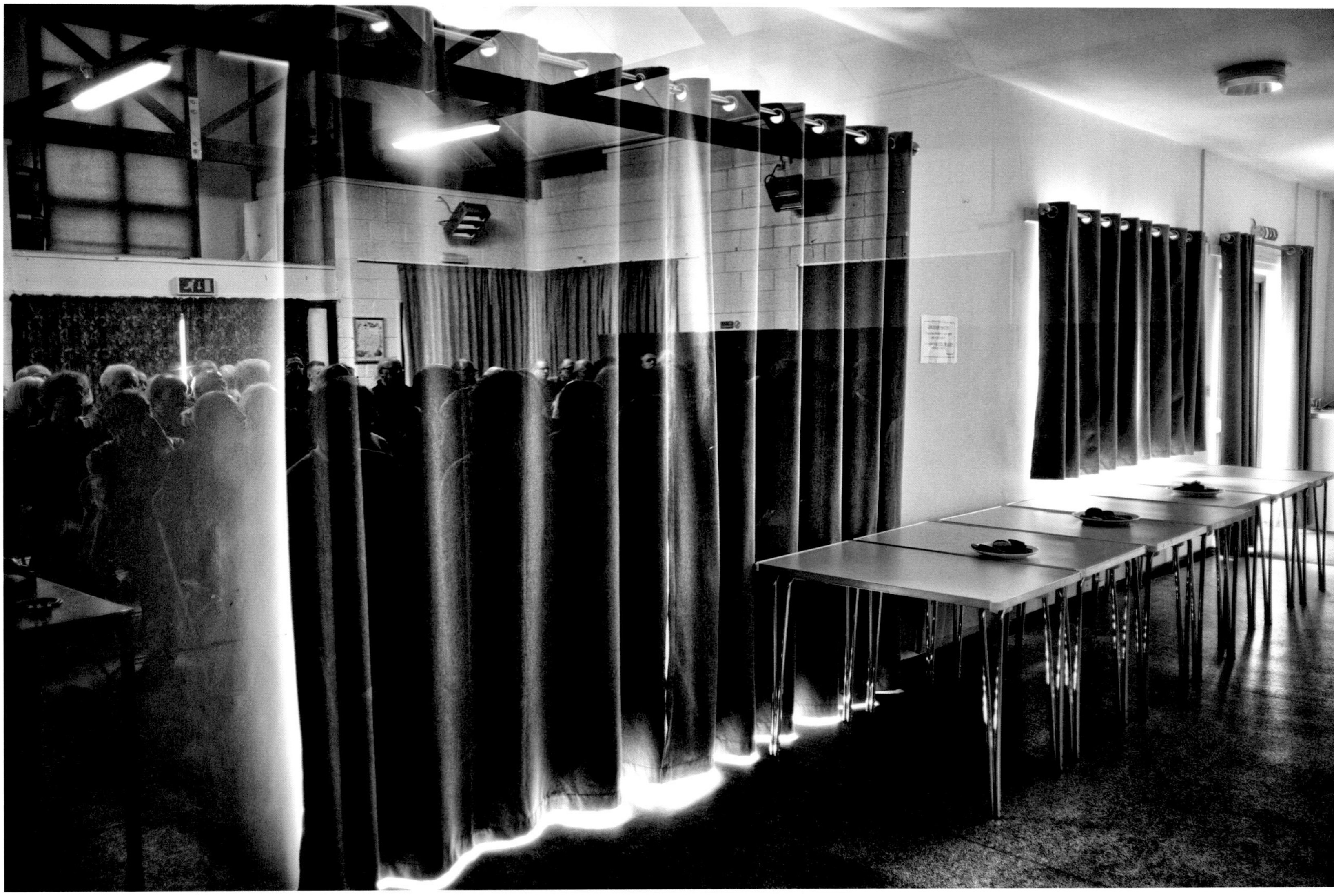

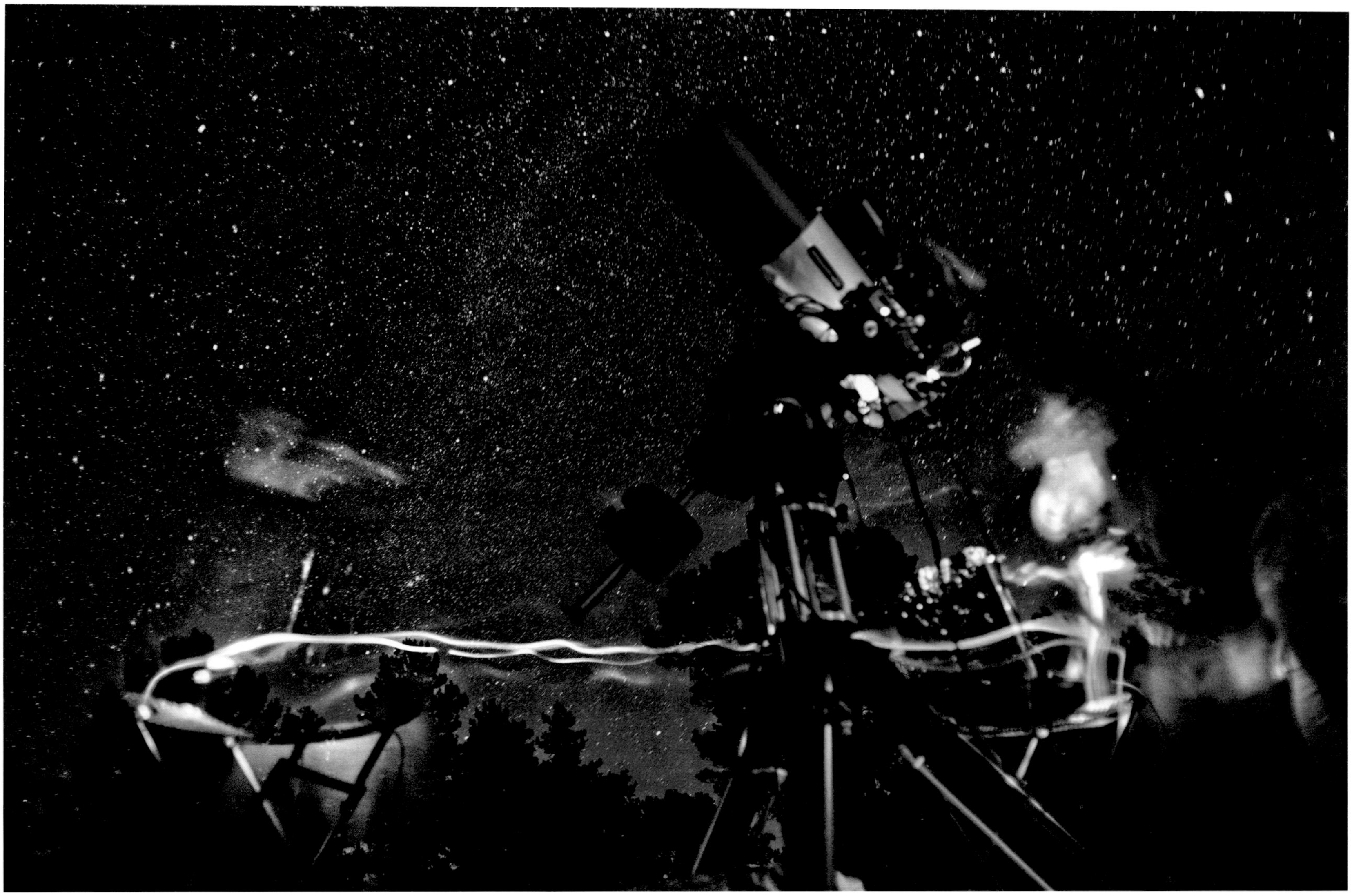

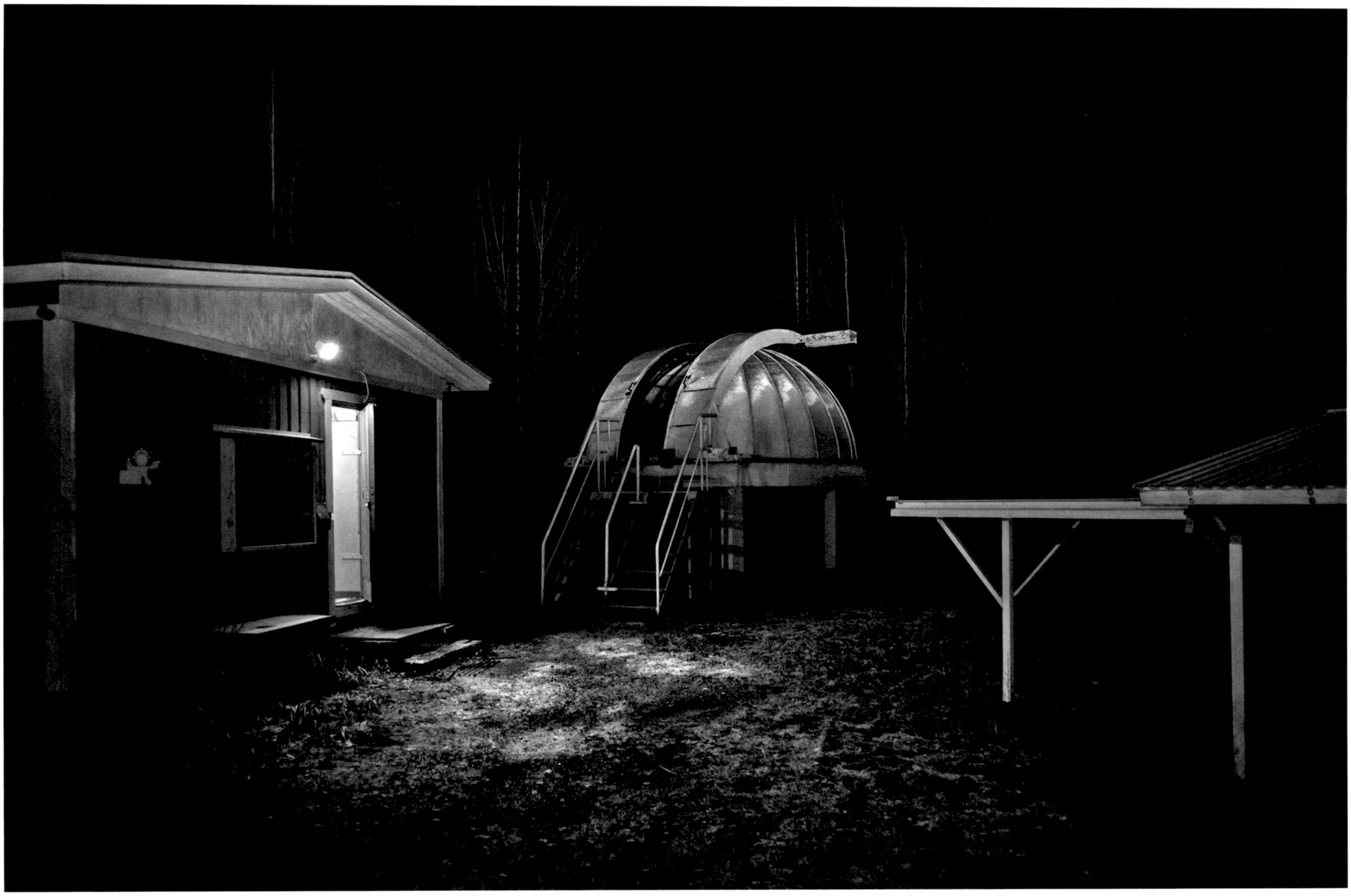

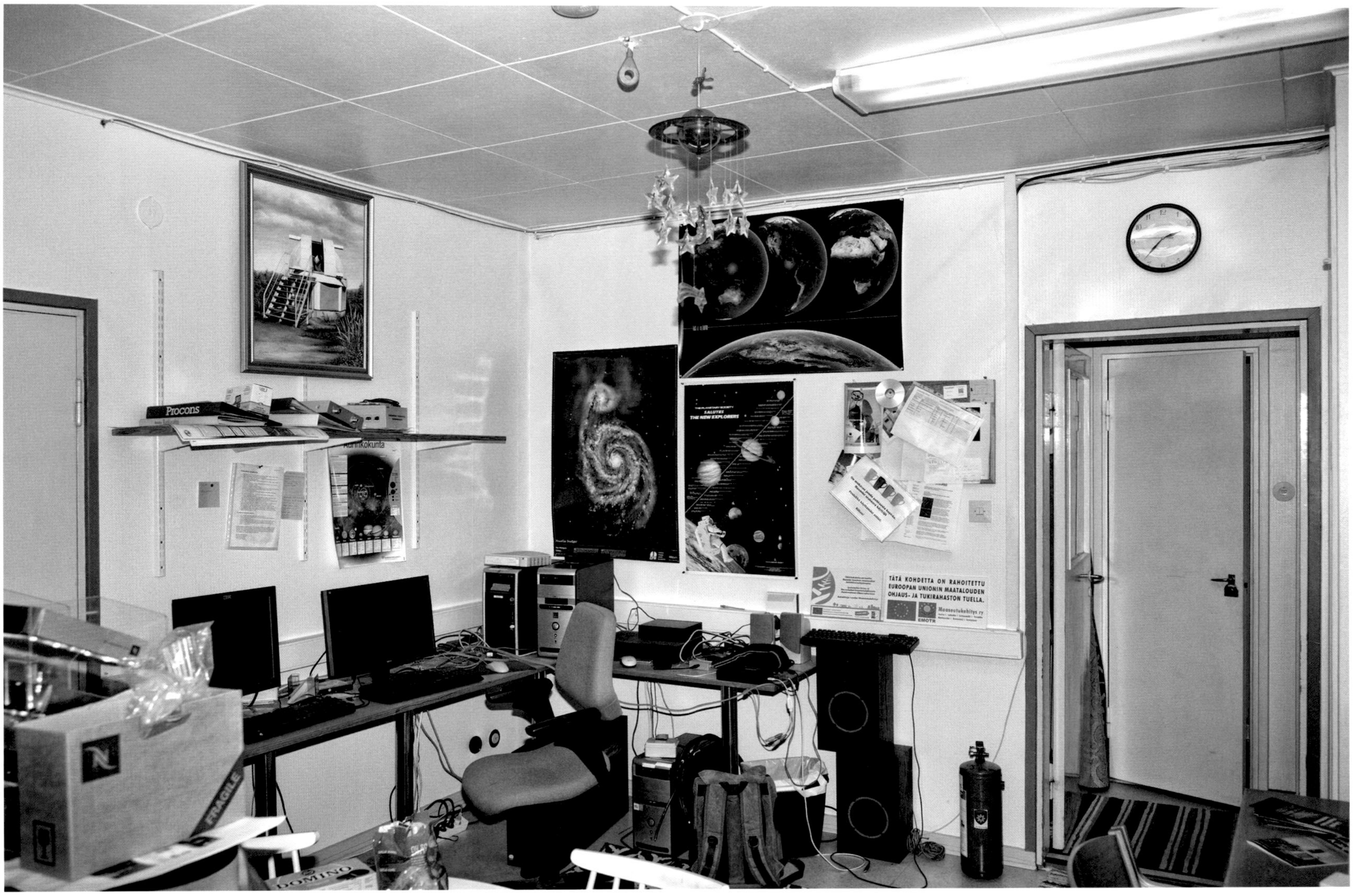
Procons
THE NEW EXPLORERS
TÄTÄ KOHDETTA ON RAHOITETTU EUROOPAN UNIONIN MAATALOUDEN OHJAUS- JA TUKIRAHASTON TUELLA.
Maaseutukehitys ry
EMOTR
FRAGILE
DOMINO

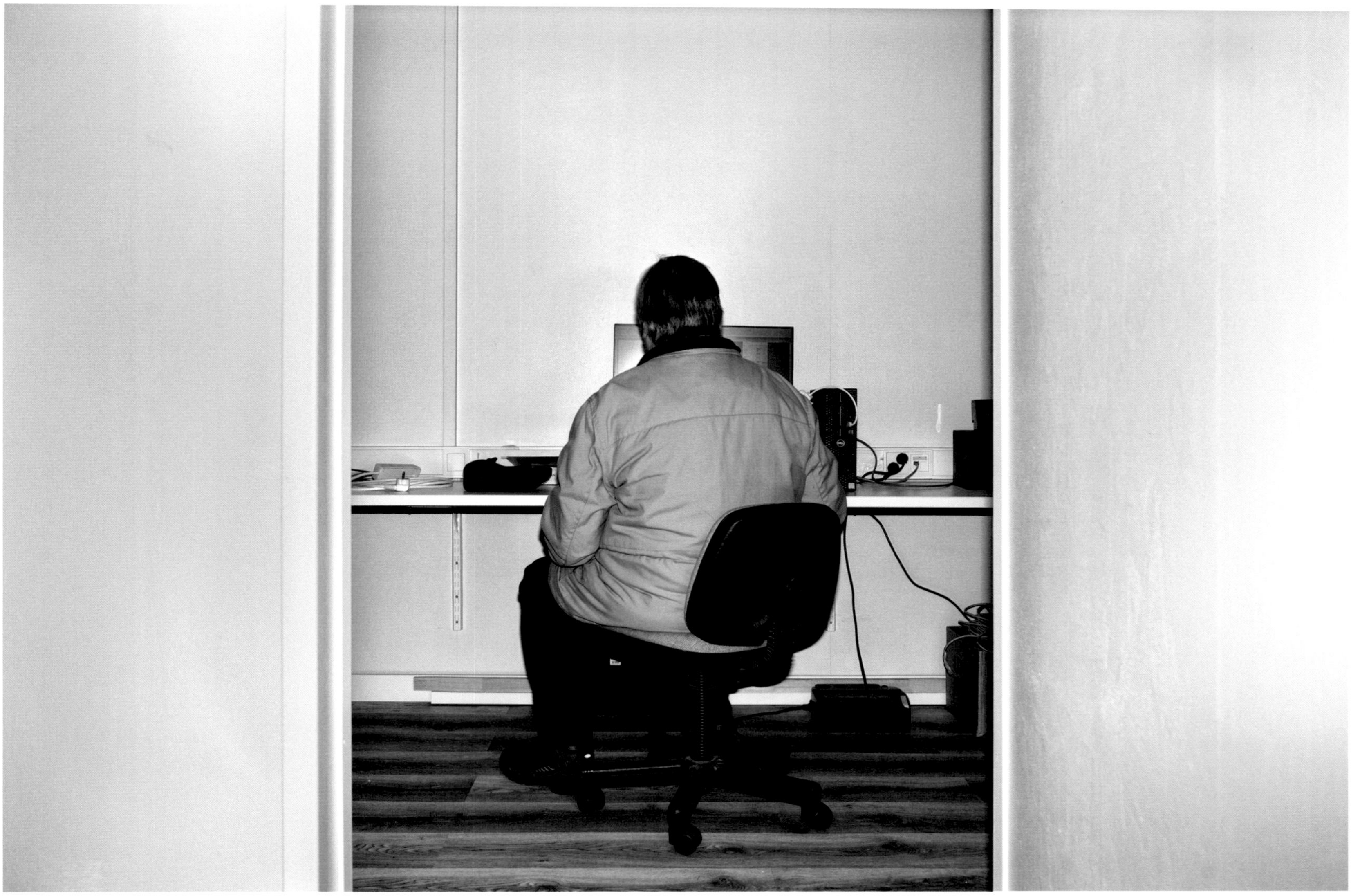

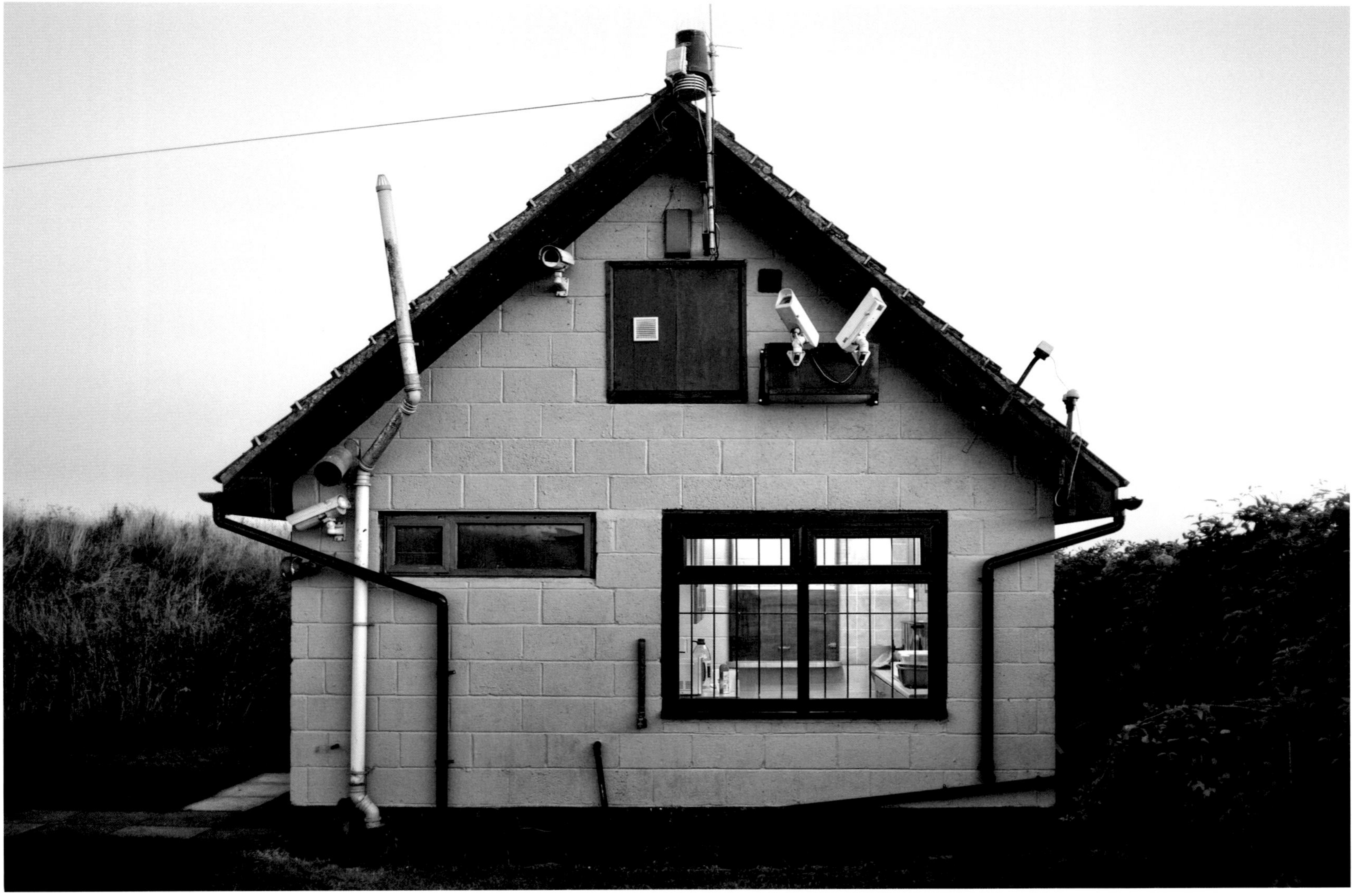

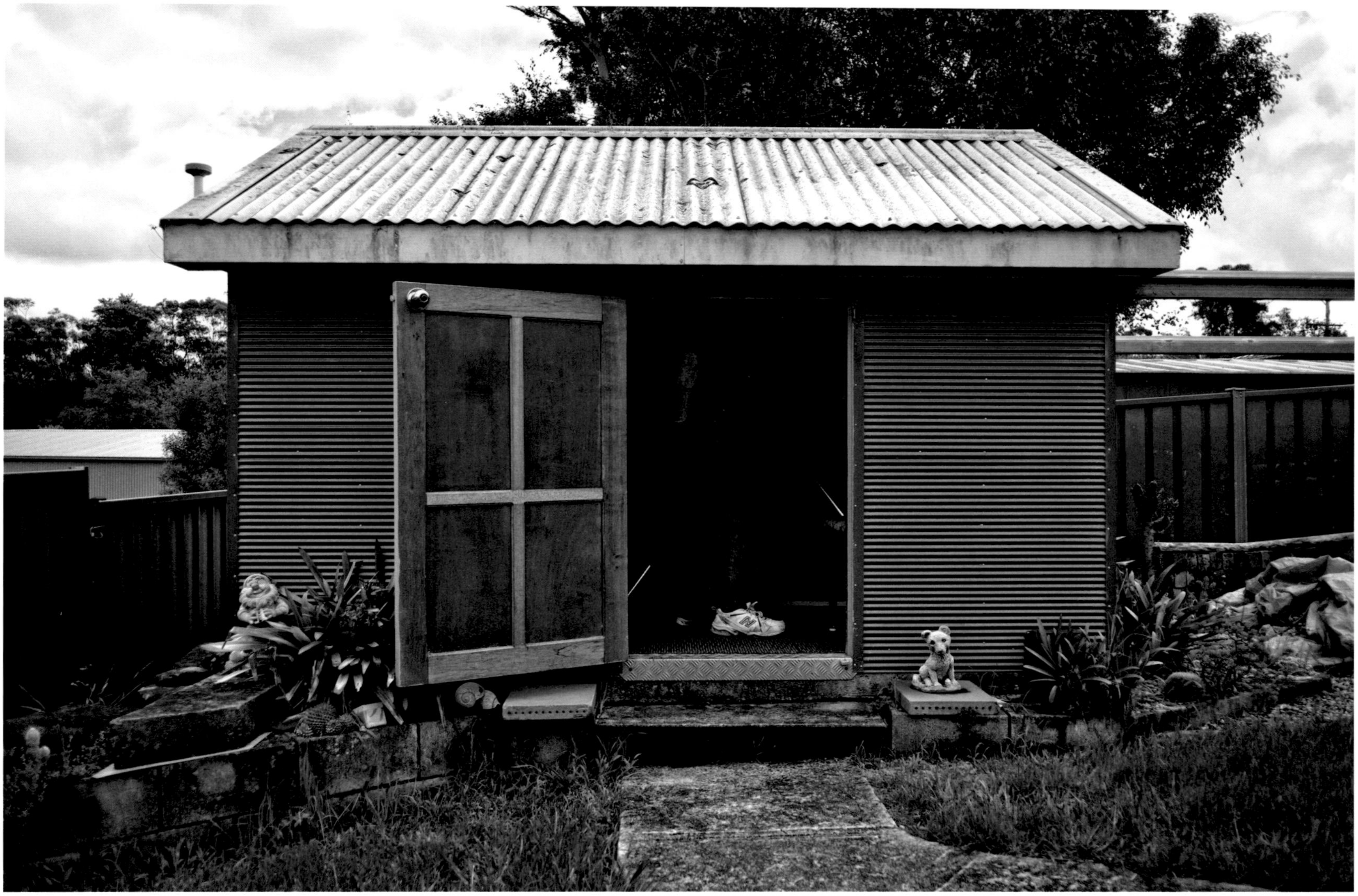

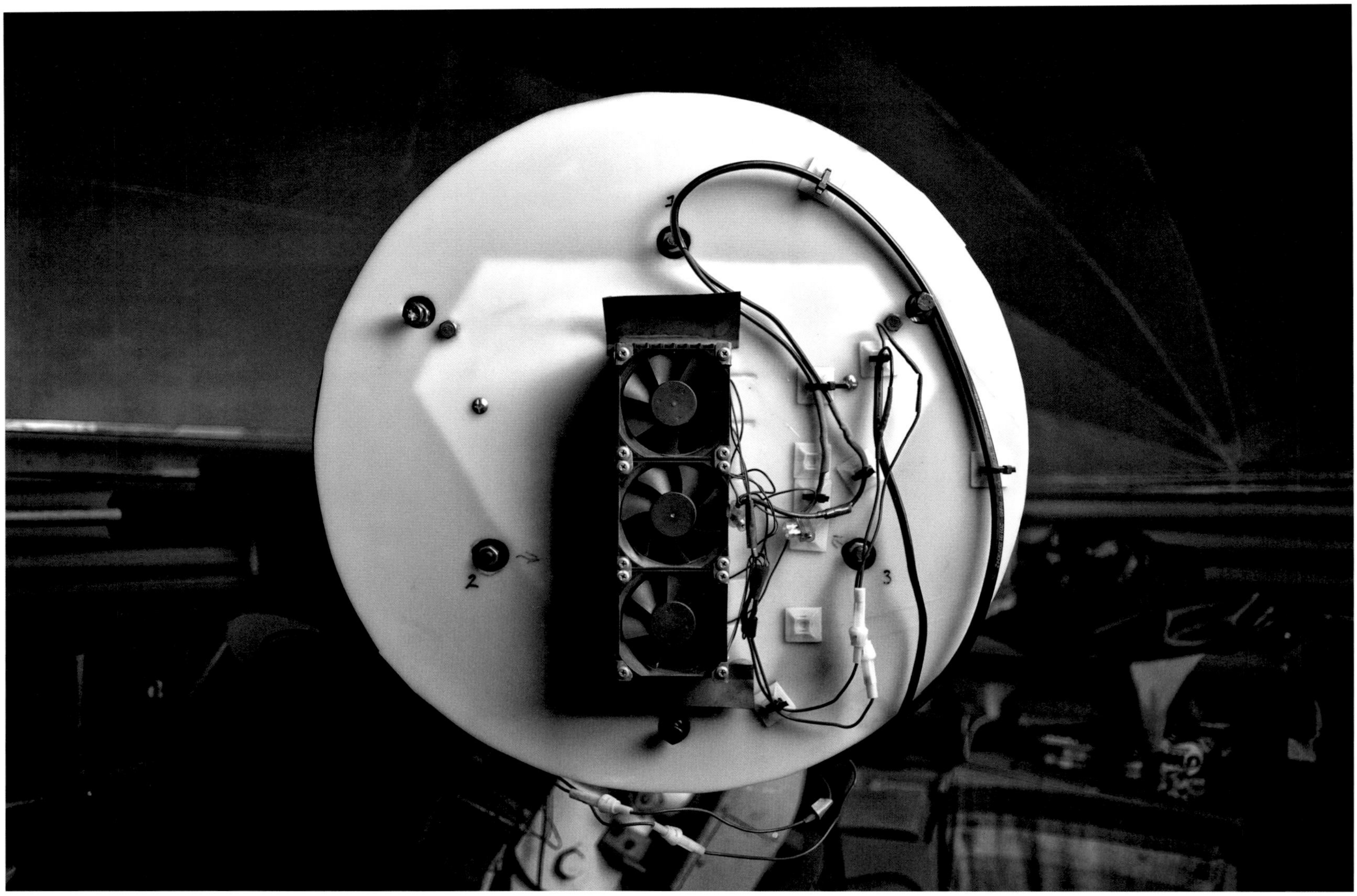

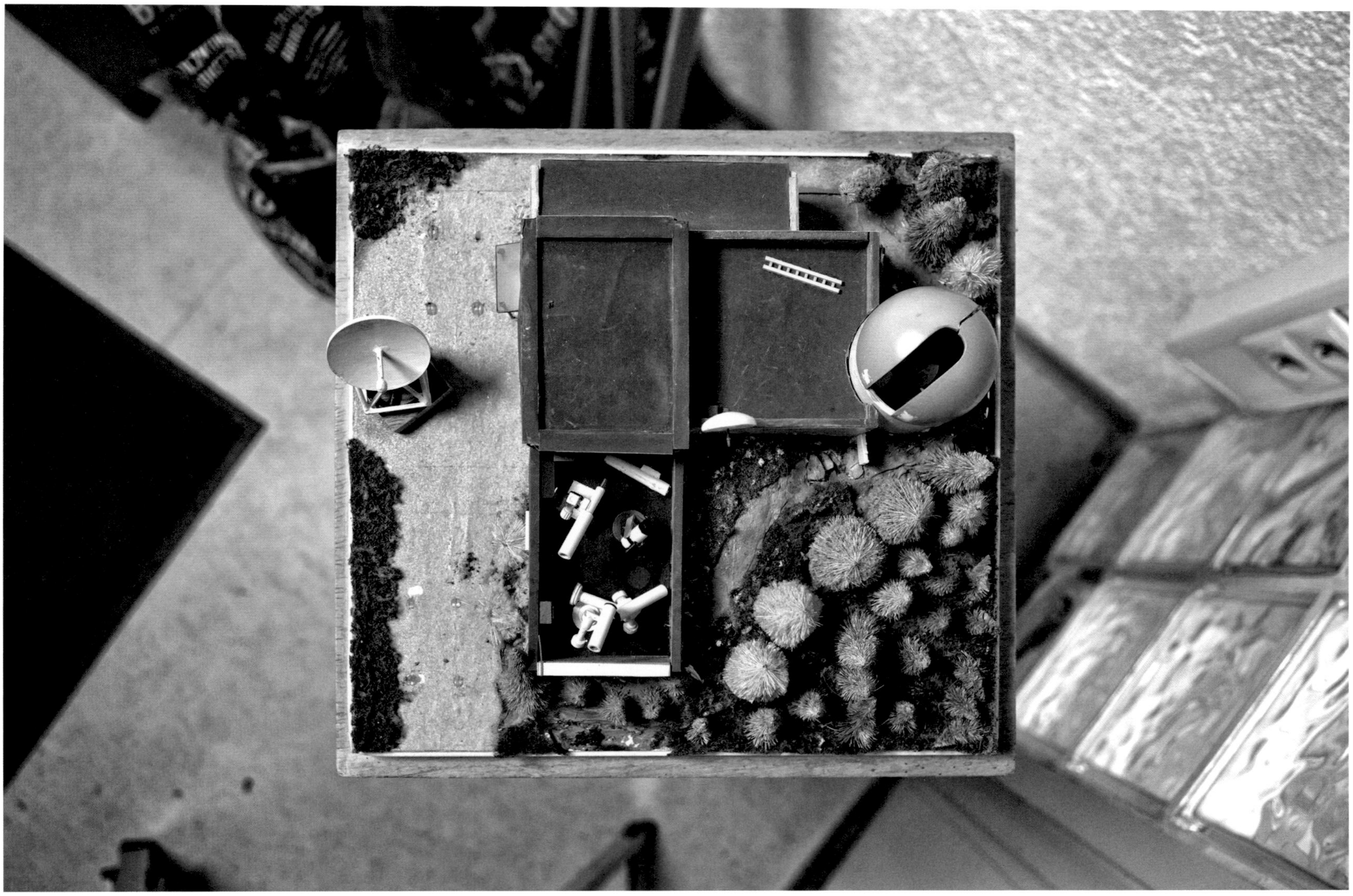

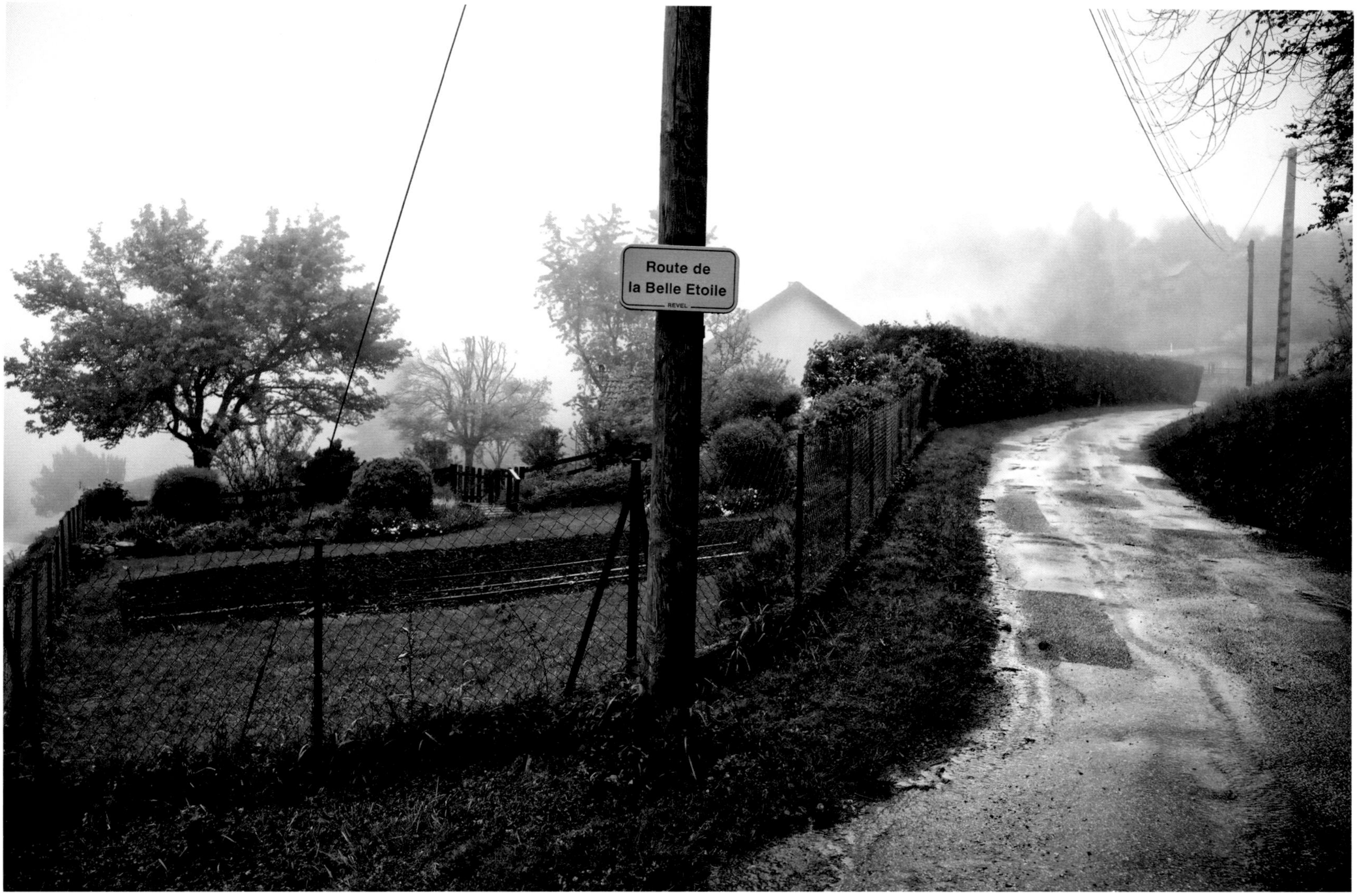
Route de
la Belle Etoile
REVEL

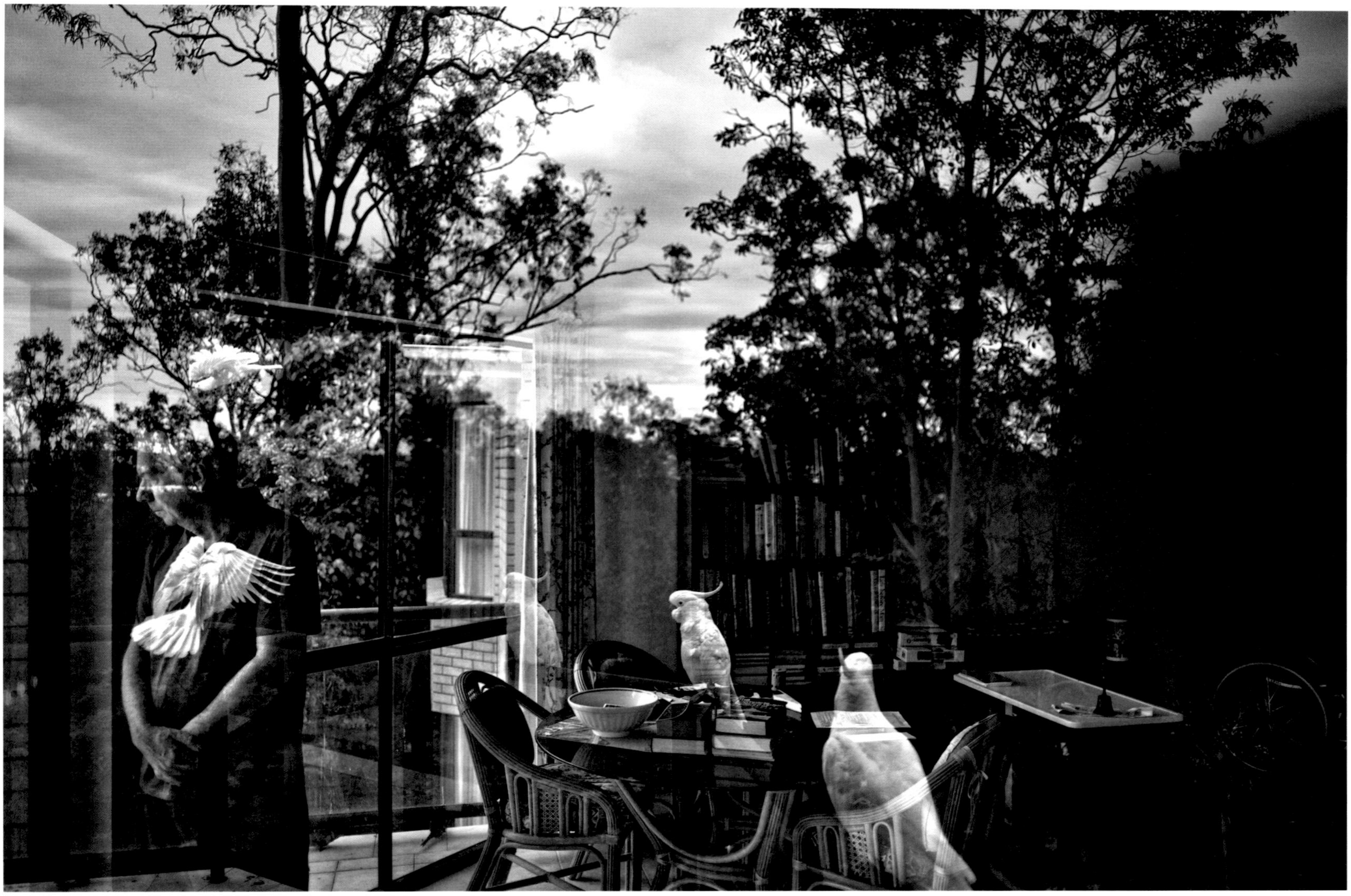

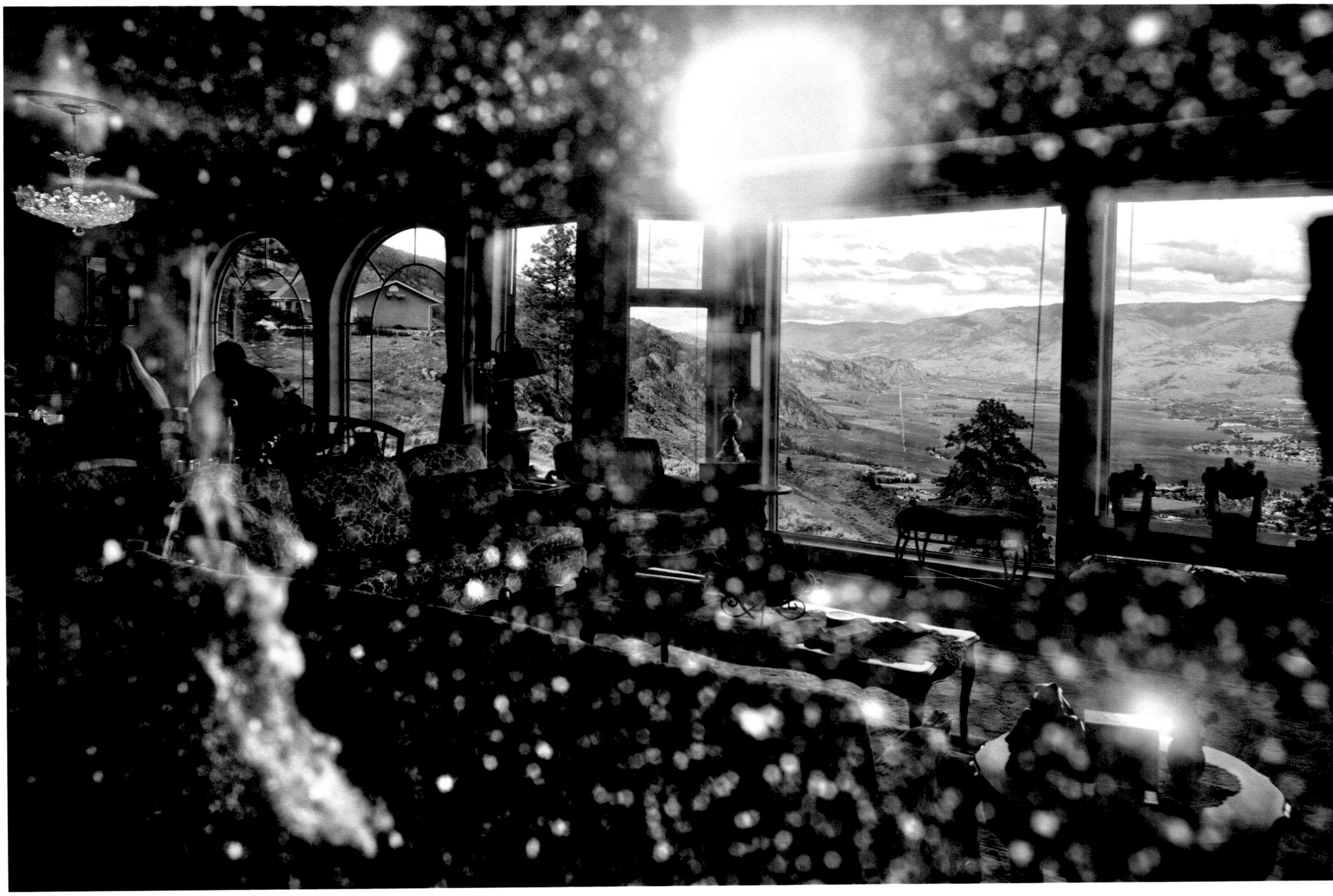

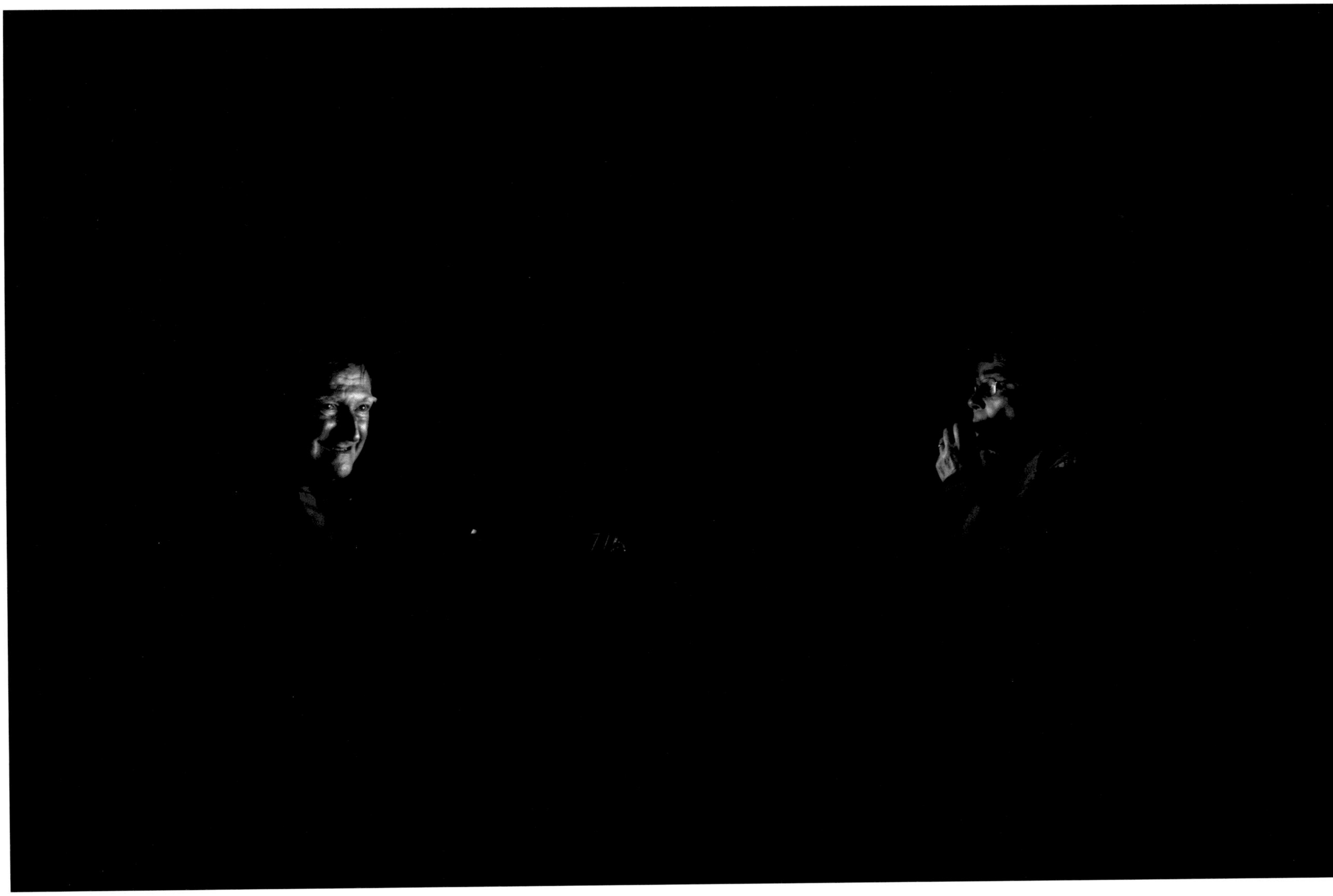

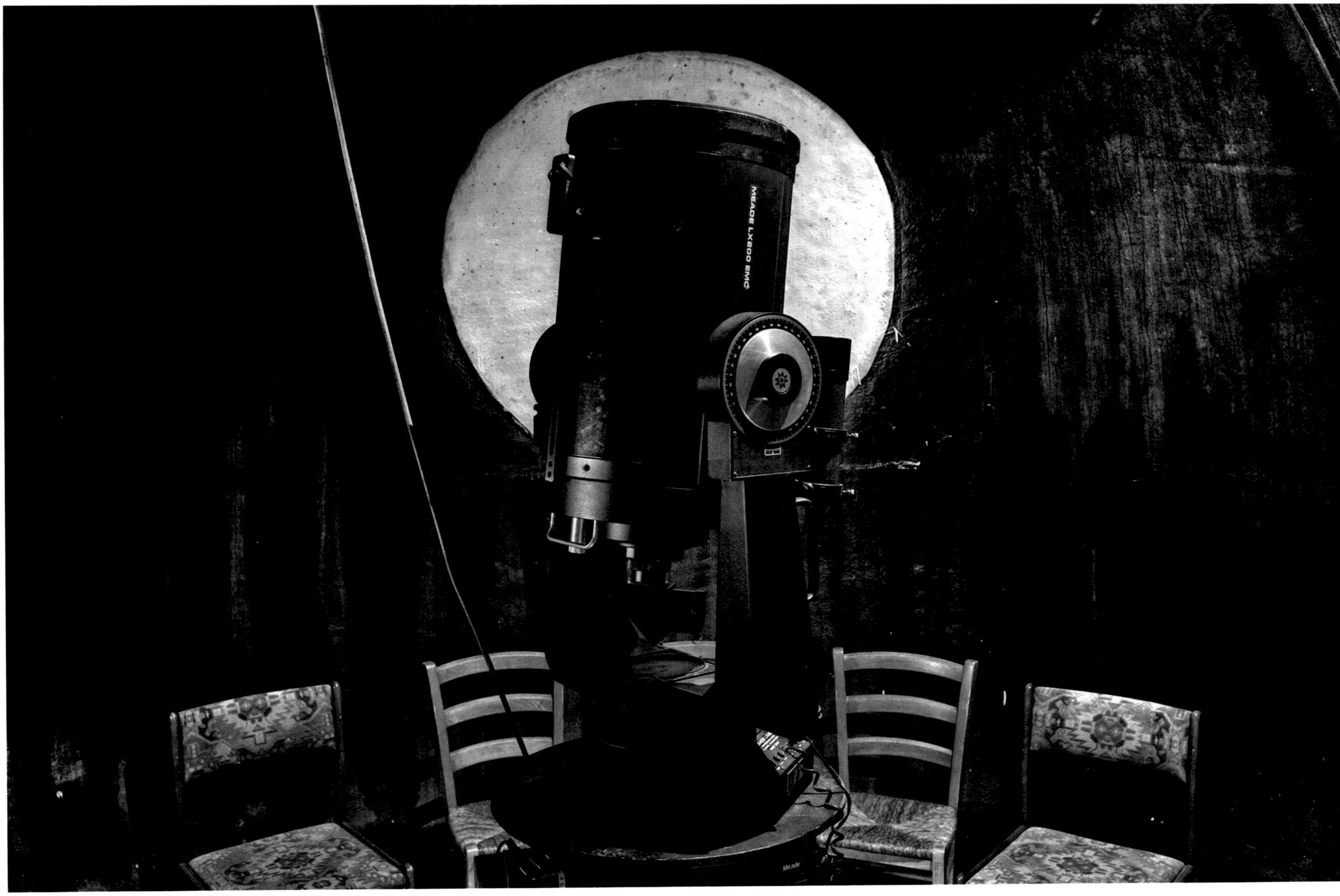
MEADE LX200 EMC
Meade

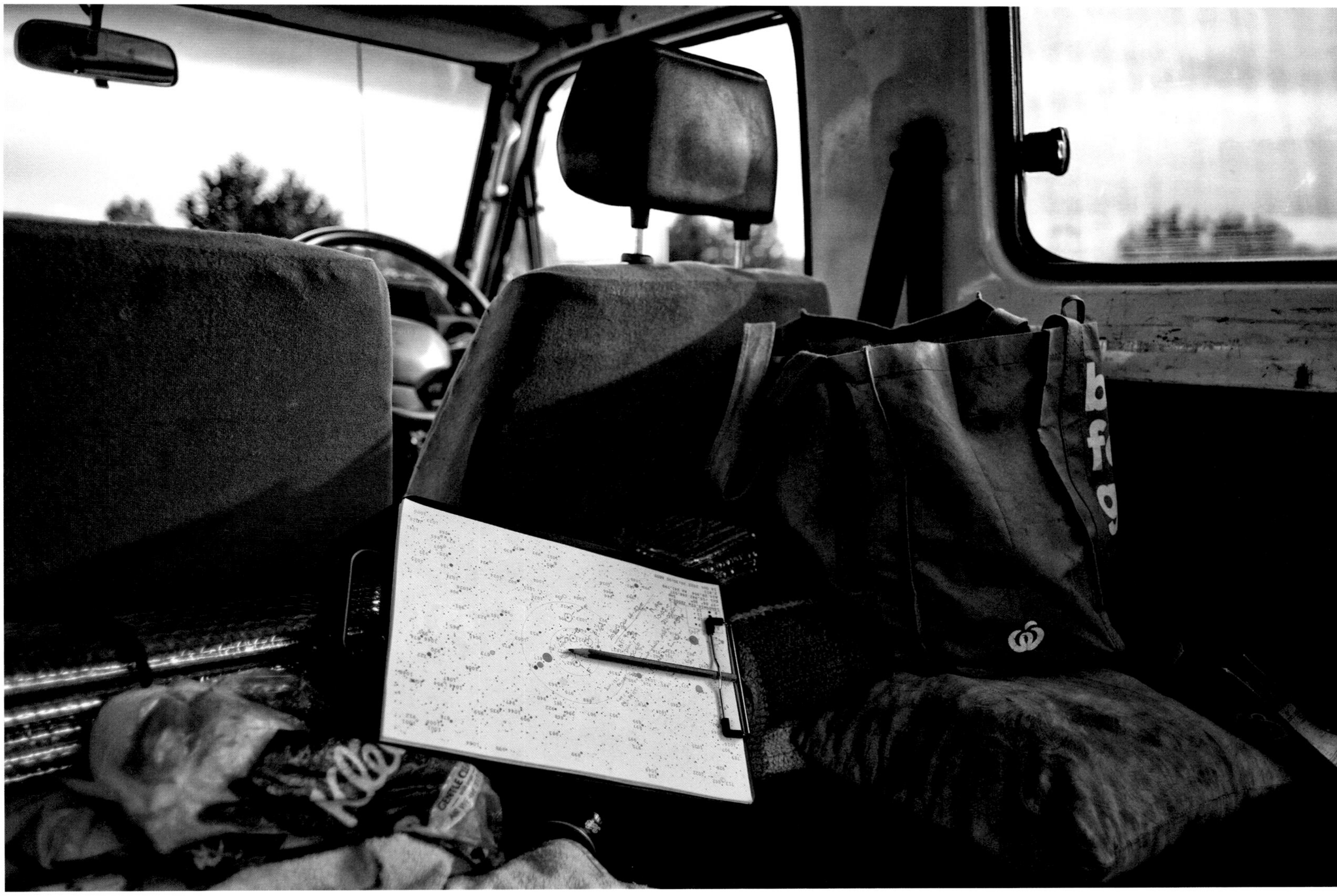

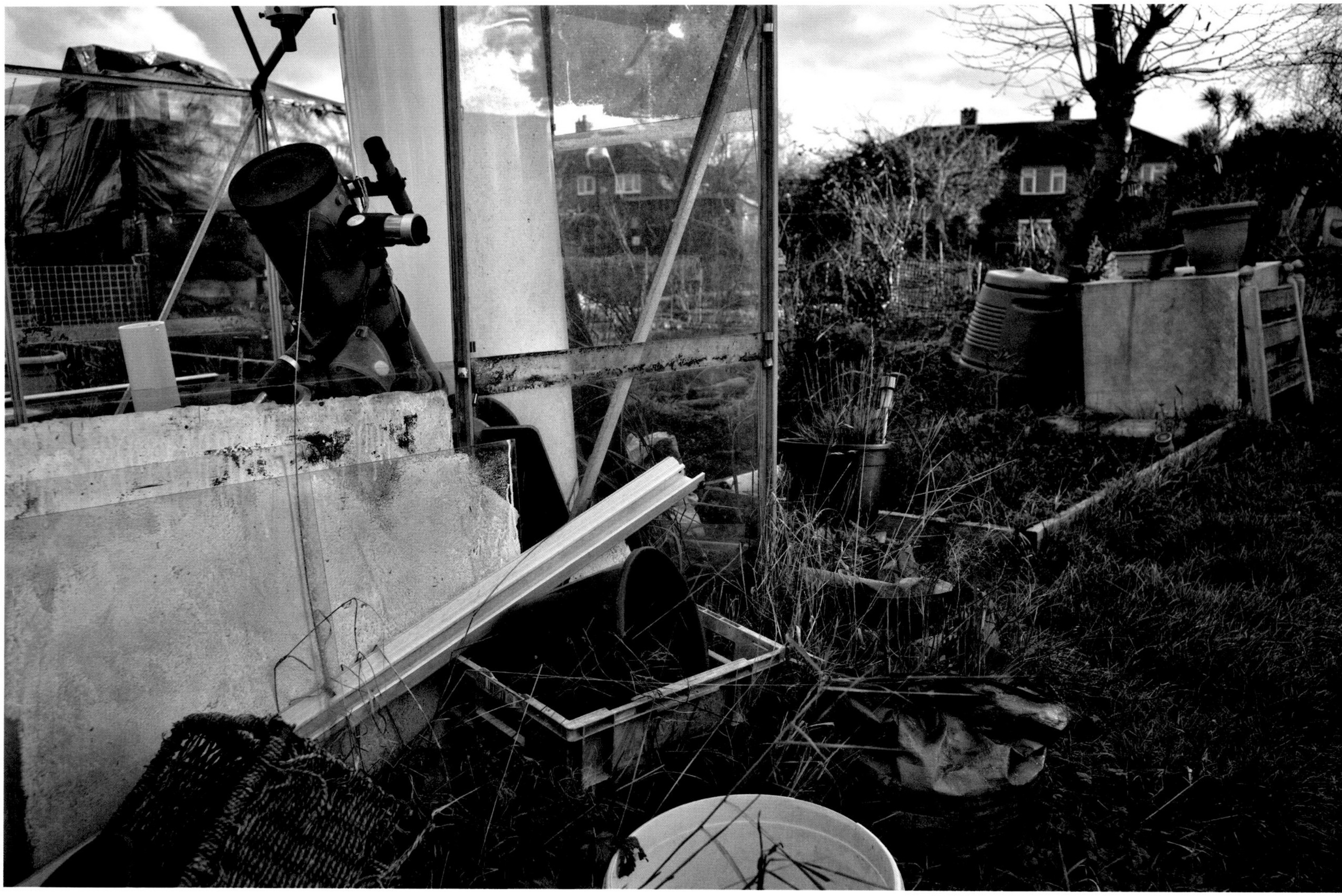

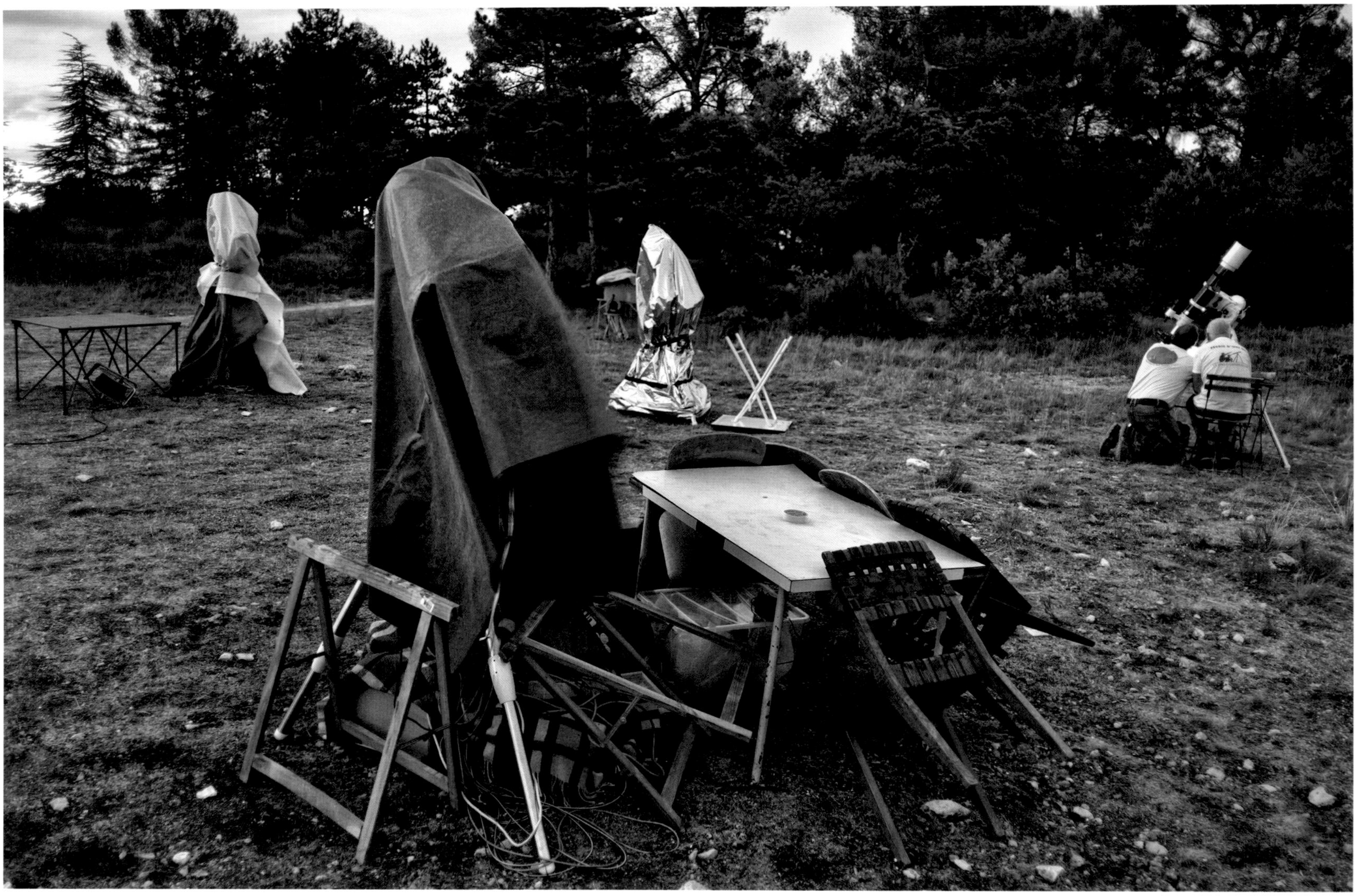

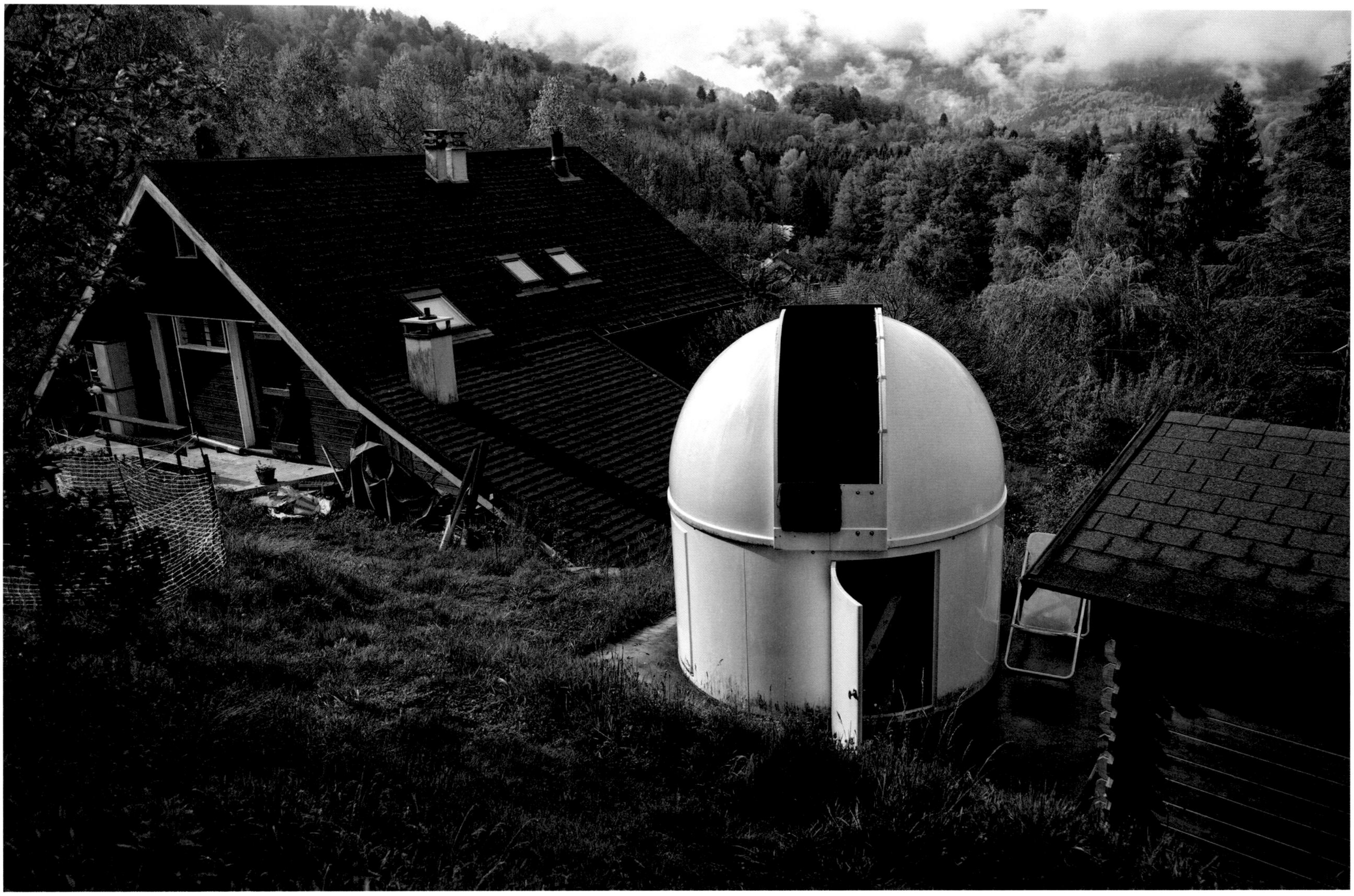

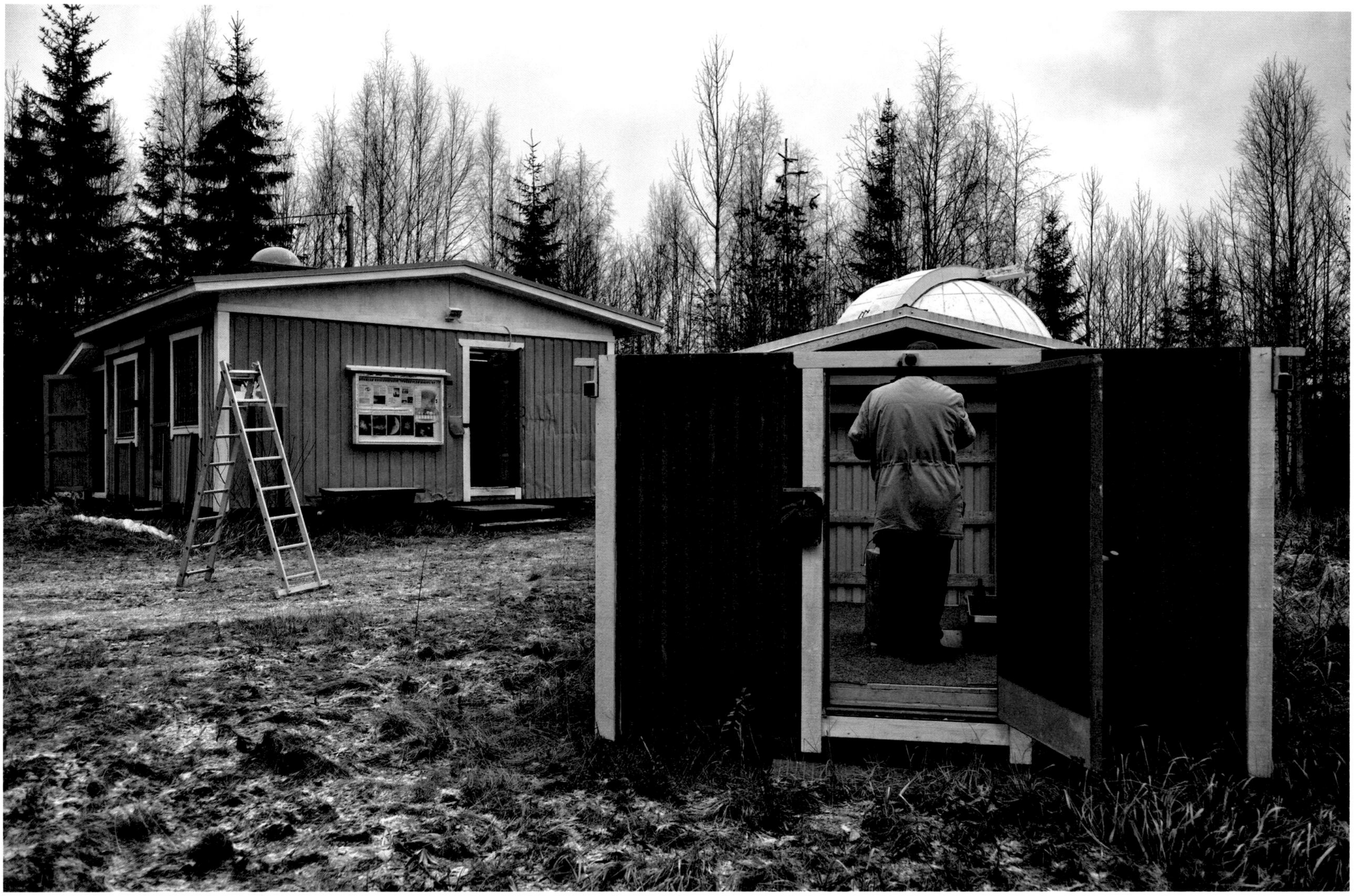

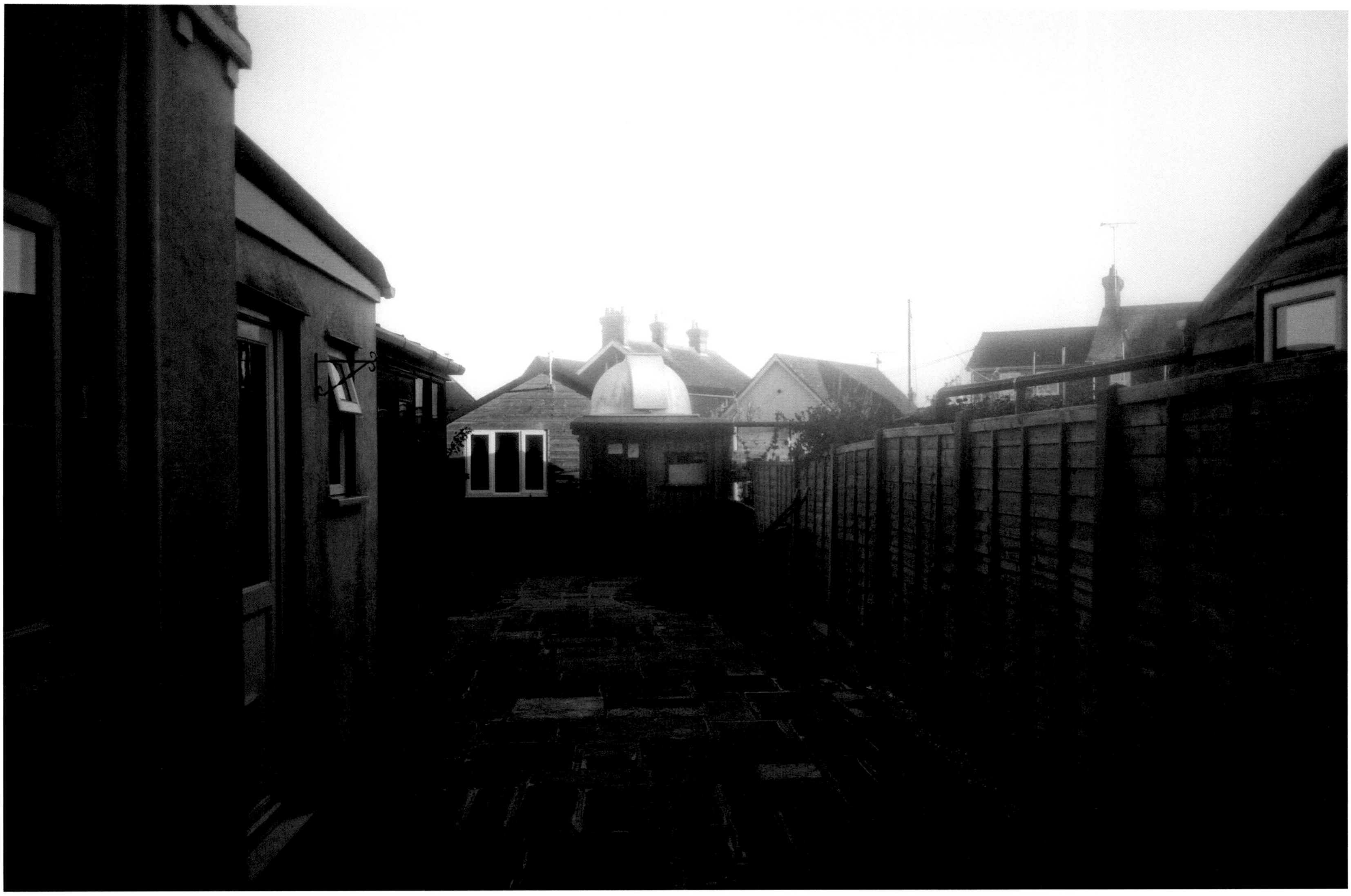

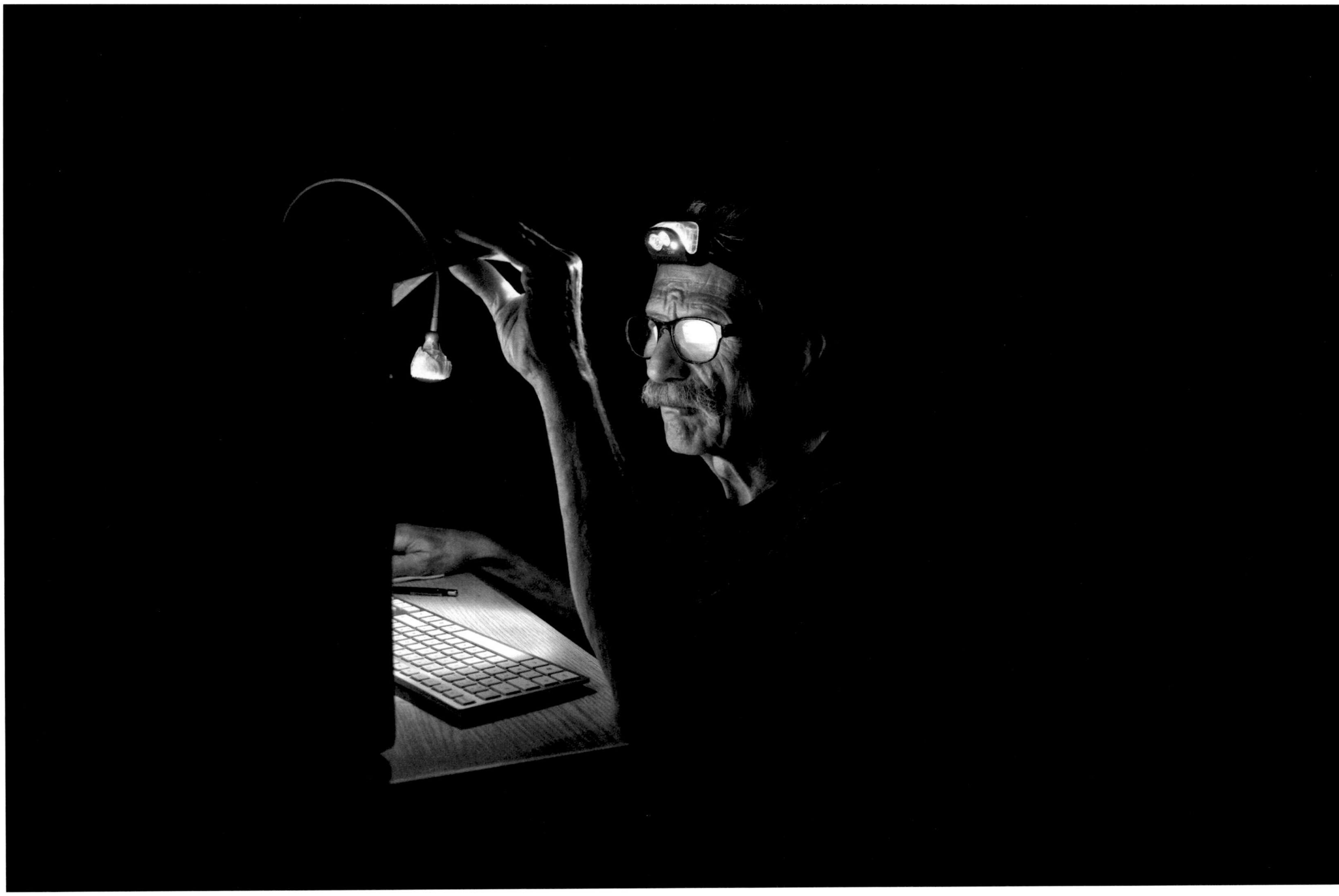

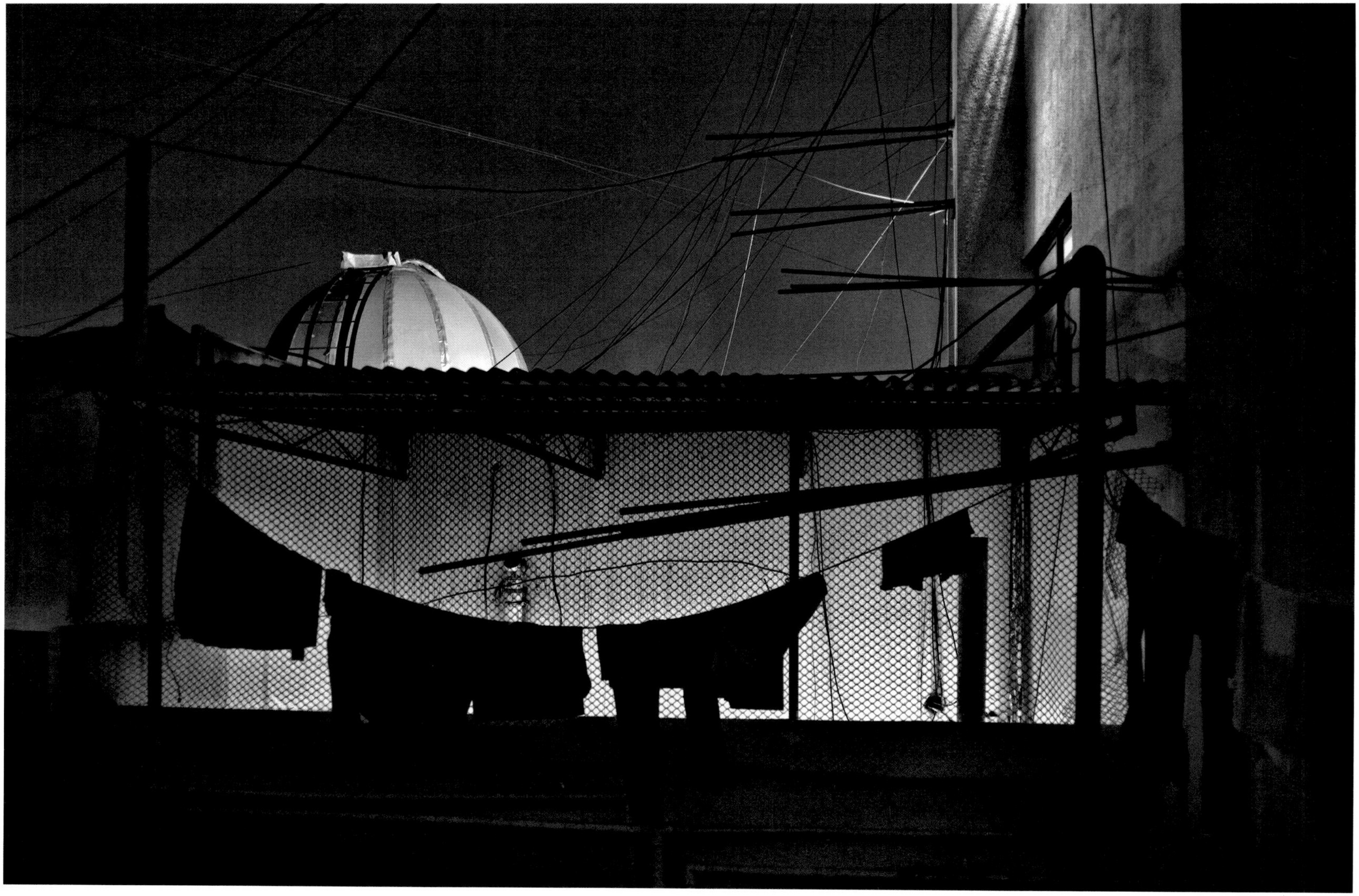

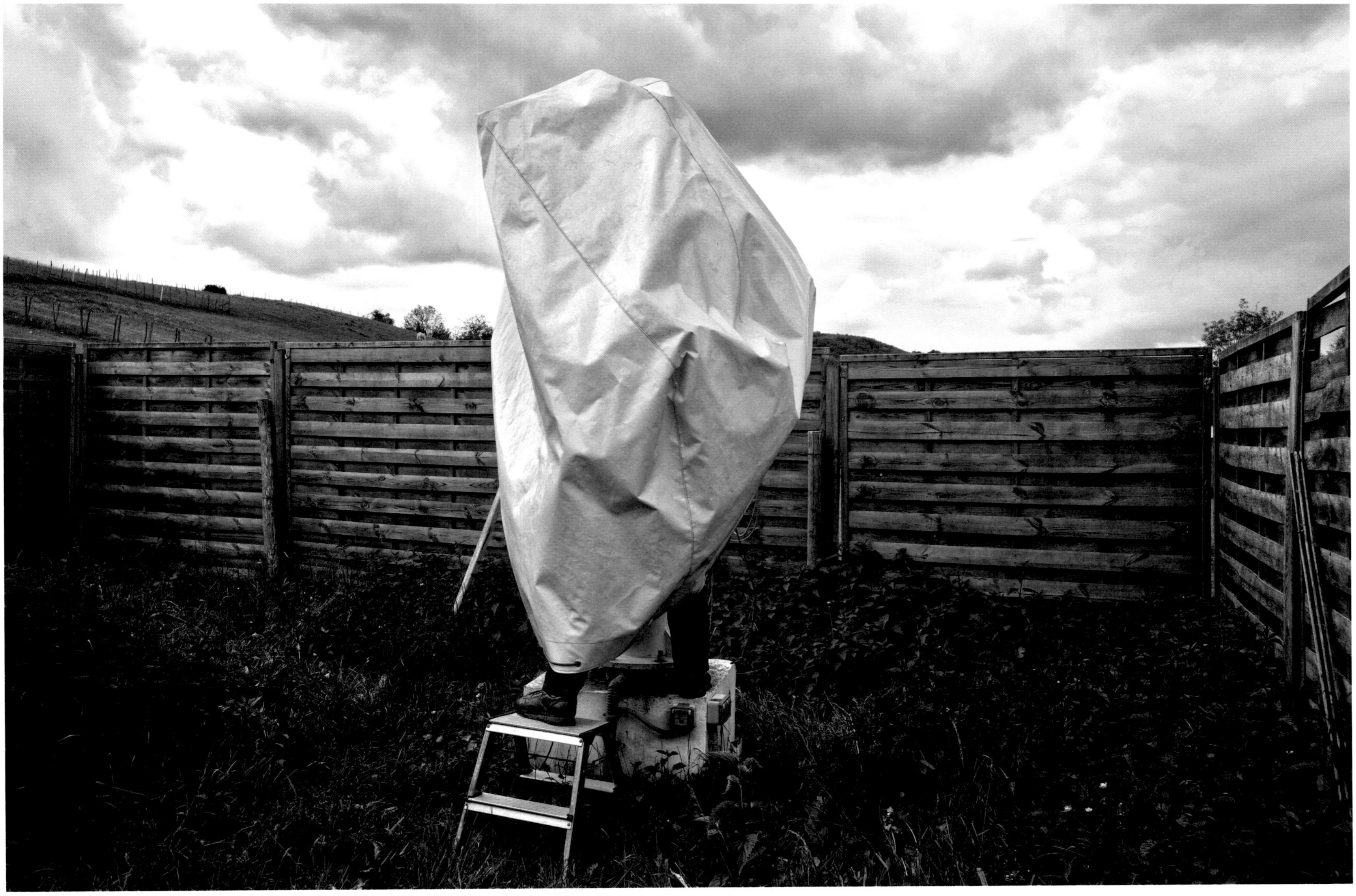

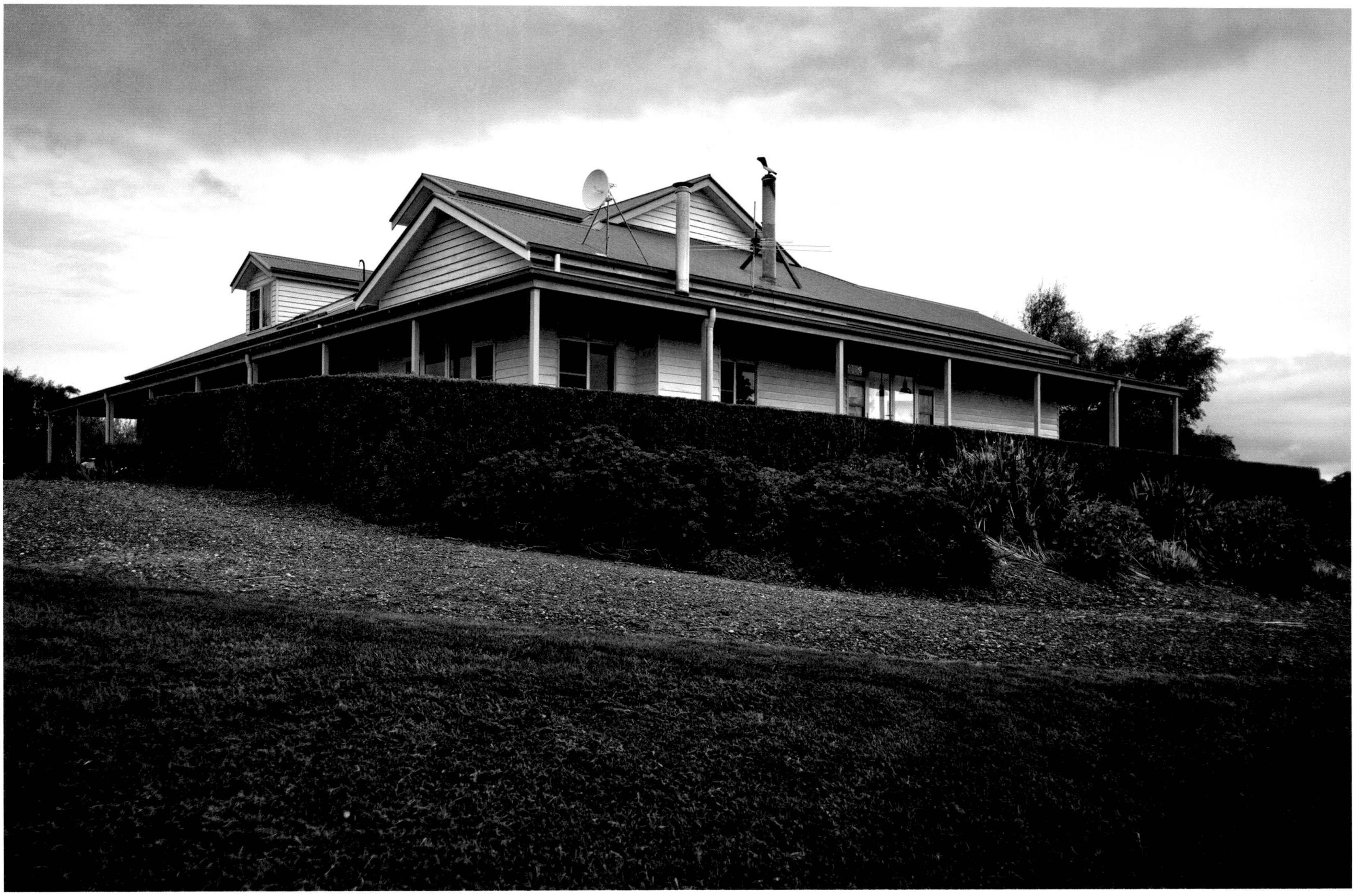

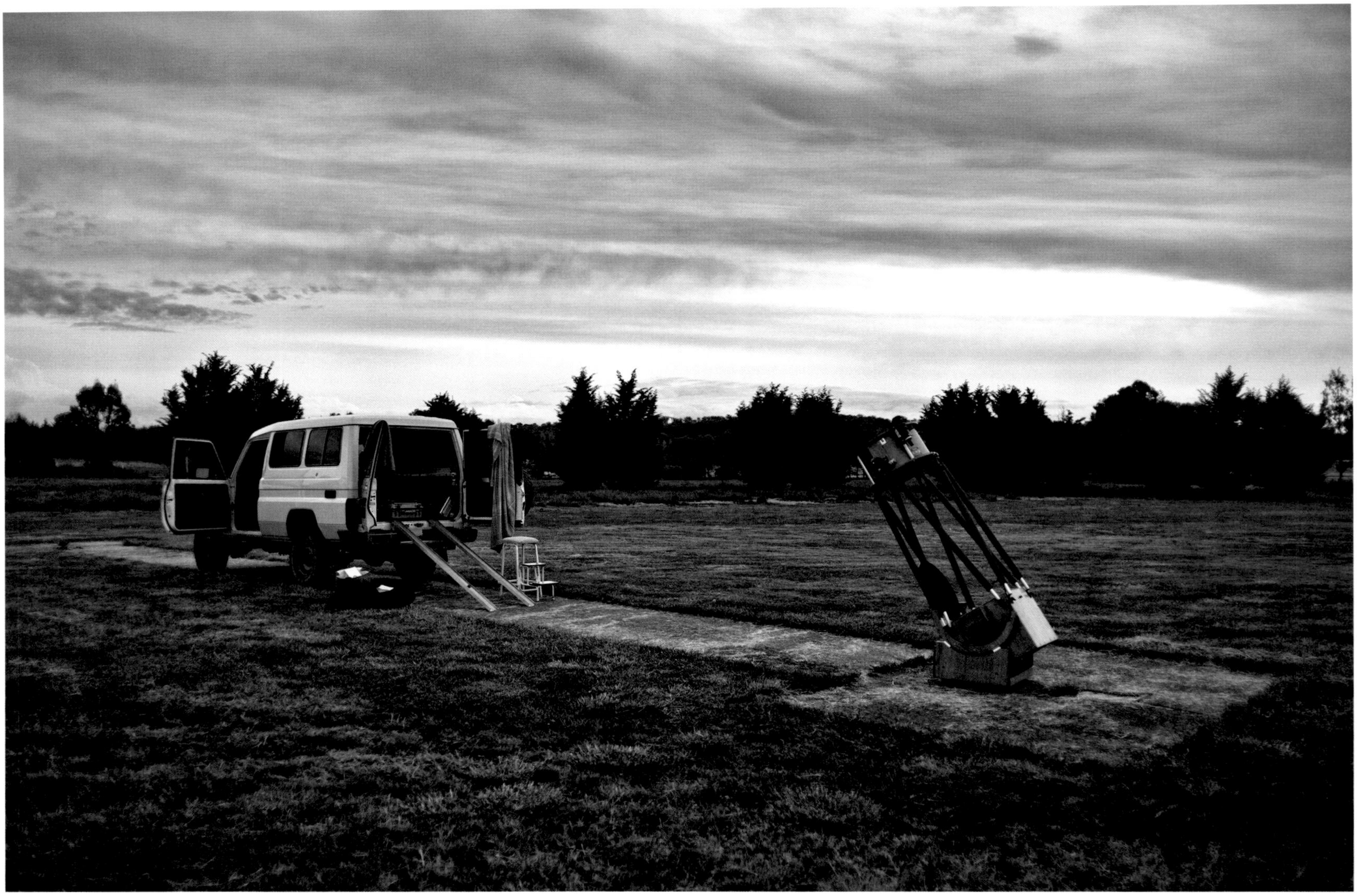

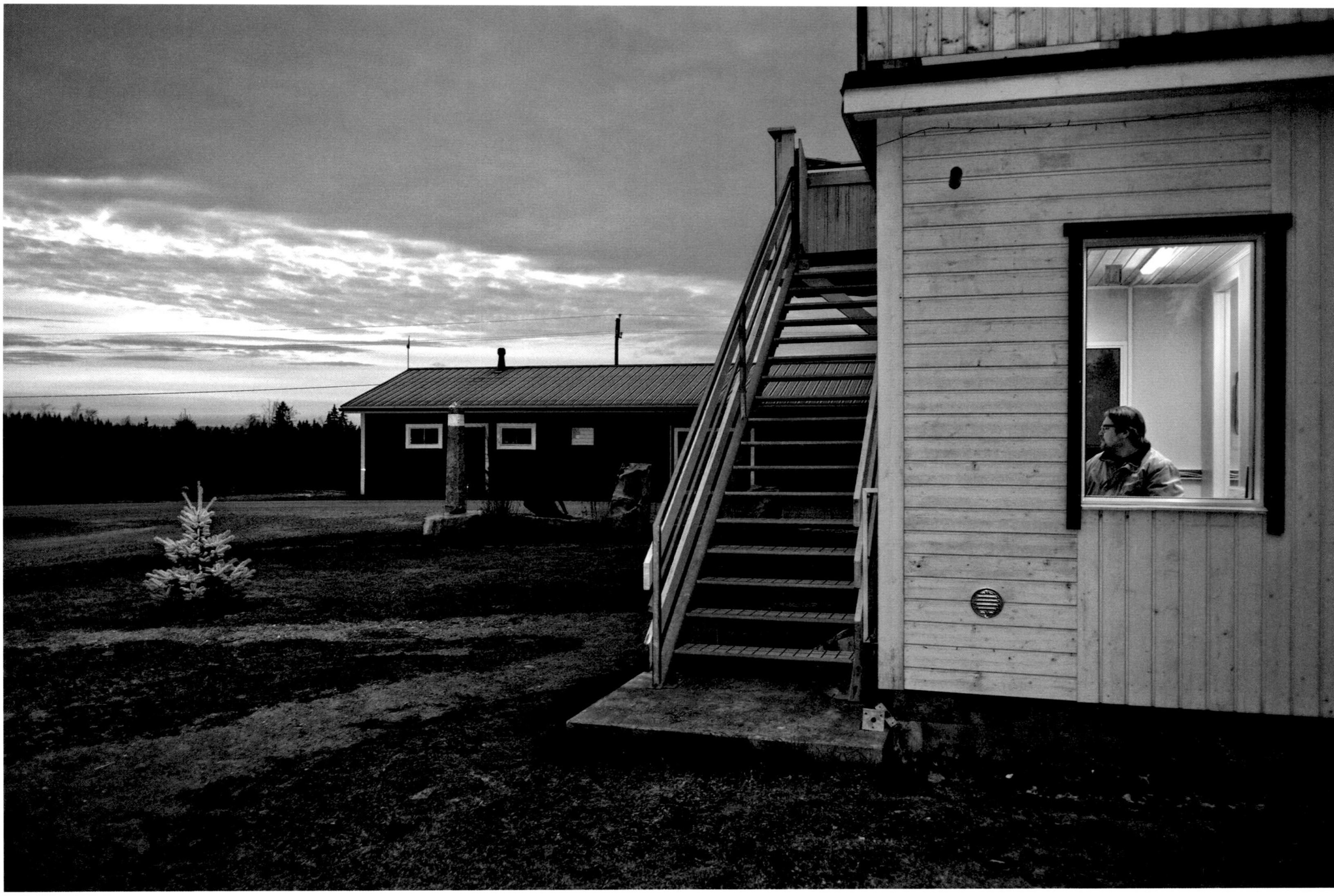

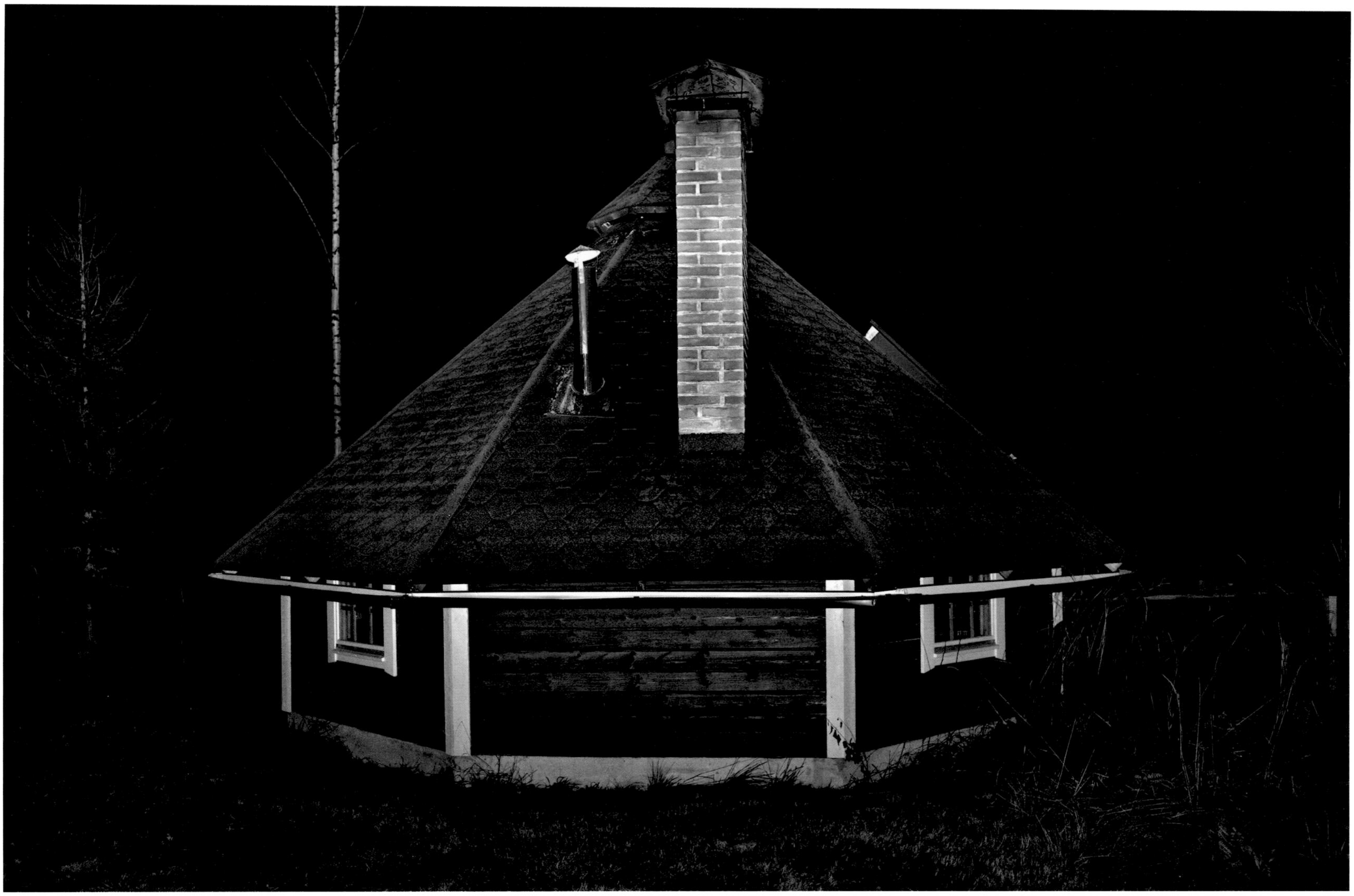

Pos-1
Pos-5
Pos-4
Pos-3
Pos-2

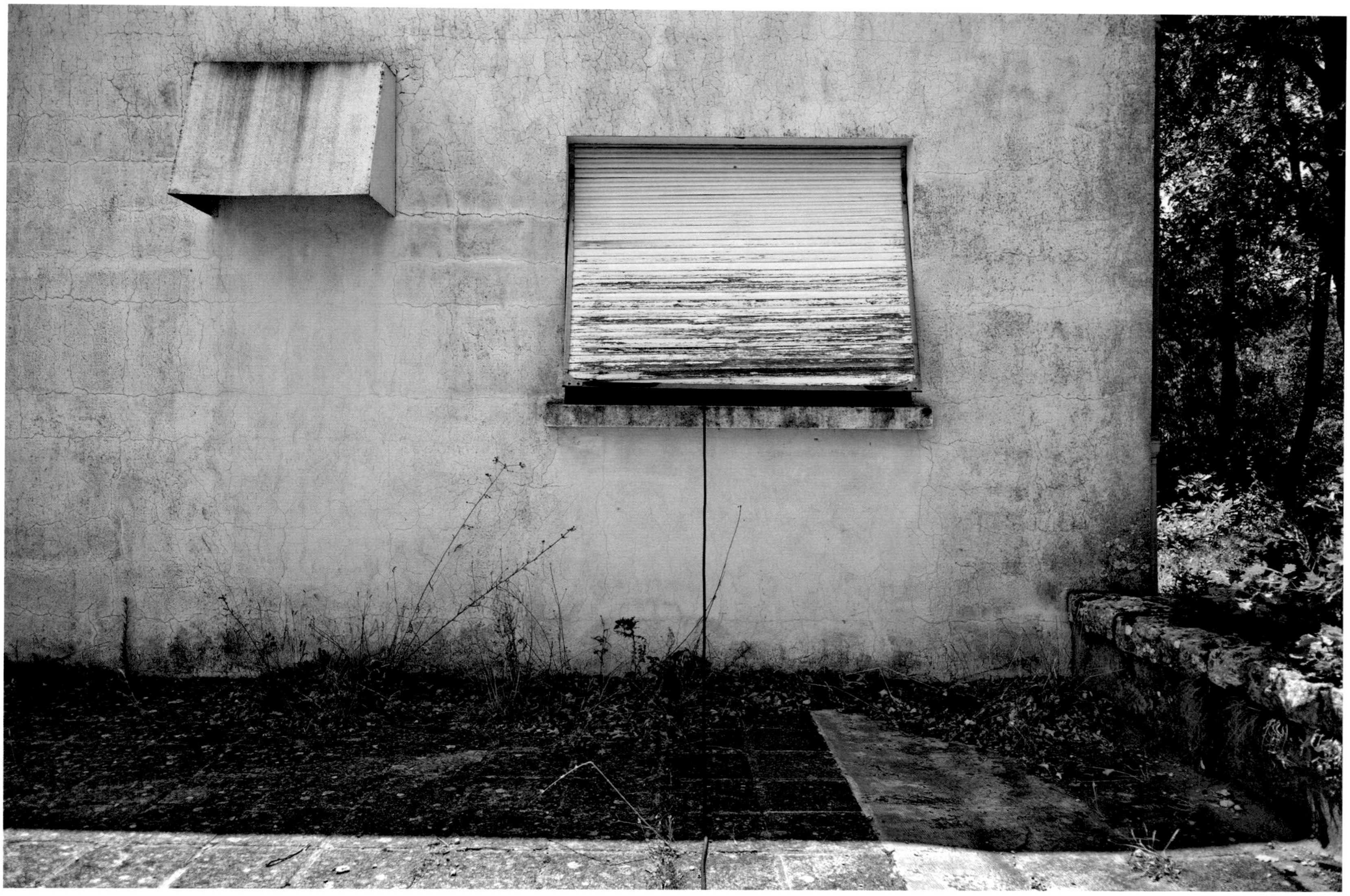

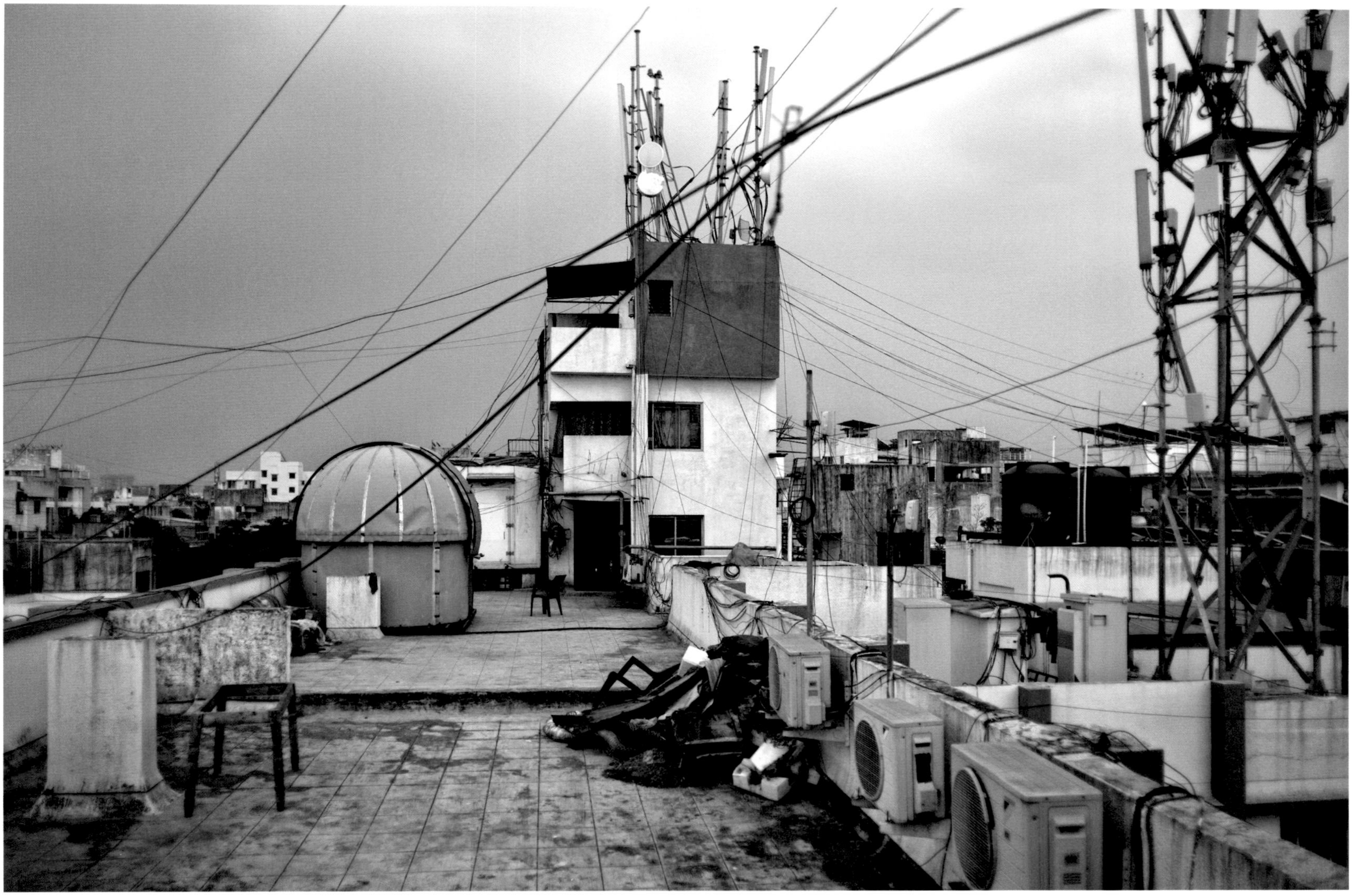

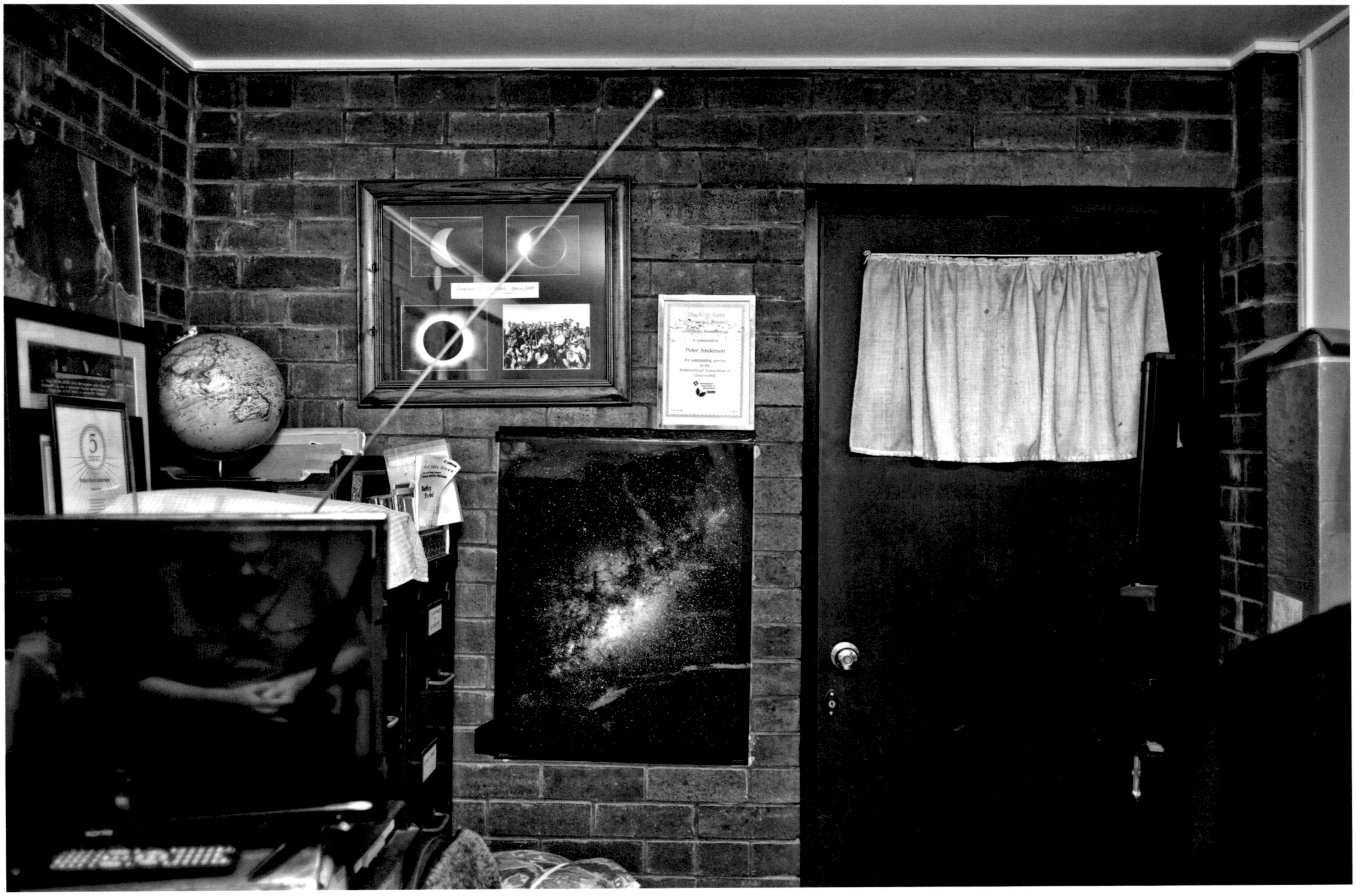
is presented to
Peter Anderson
for outstanding service
to the
Astronomical Association of
Queensland

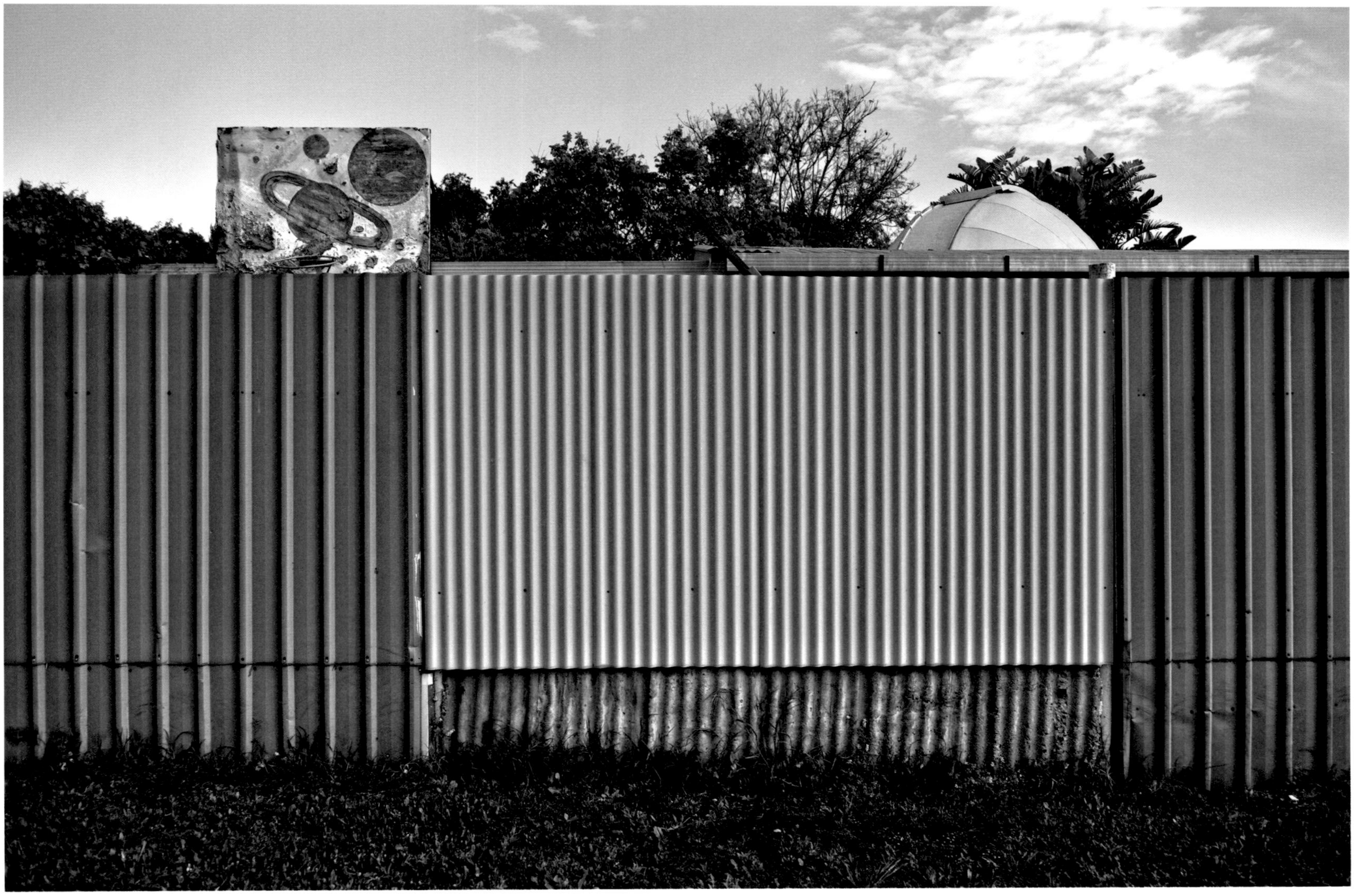

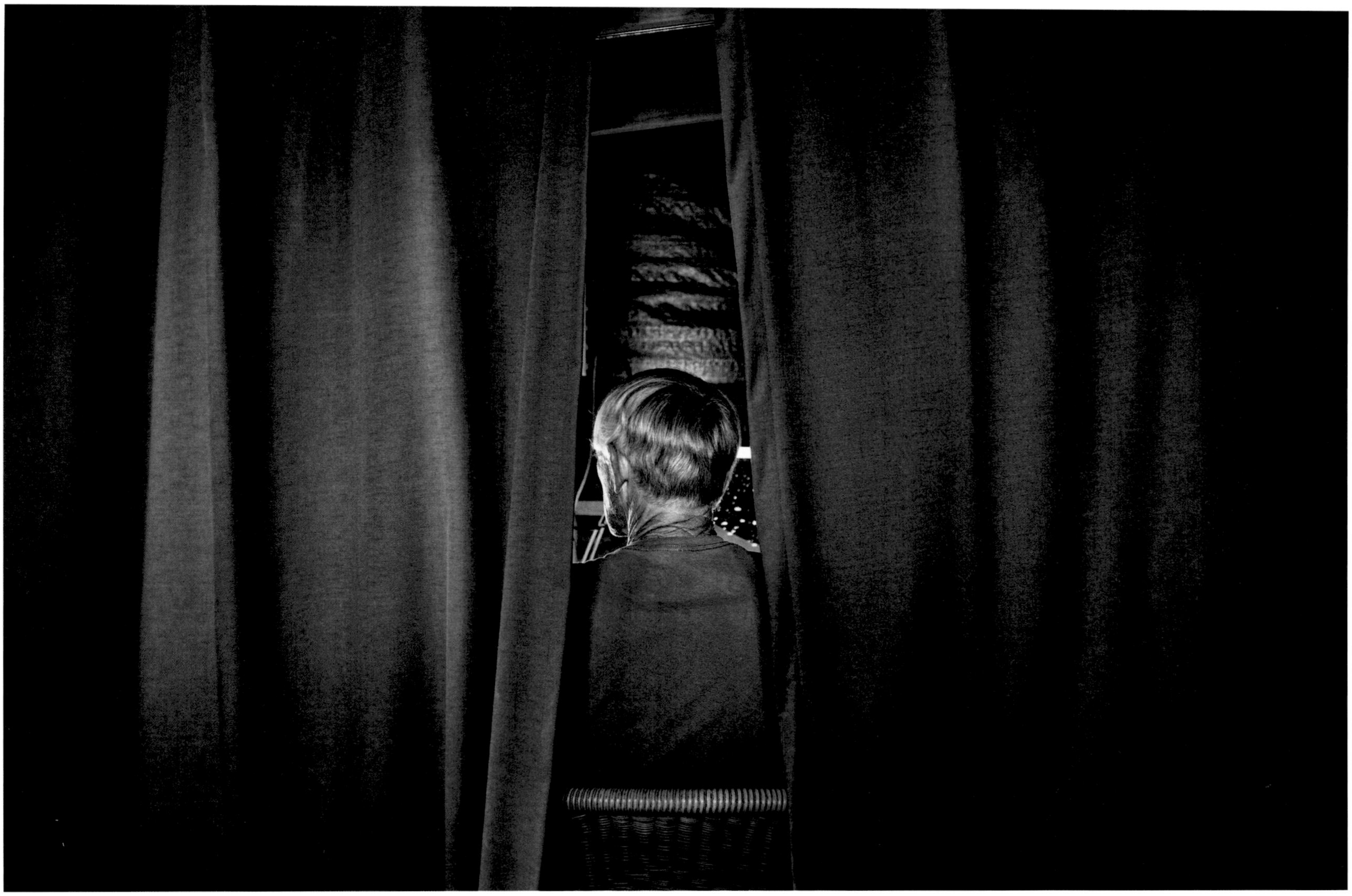

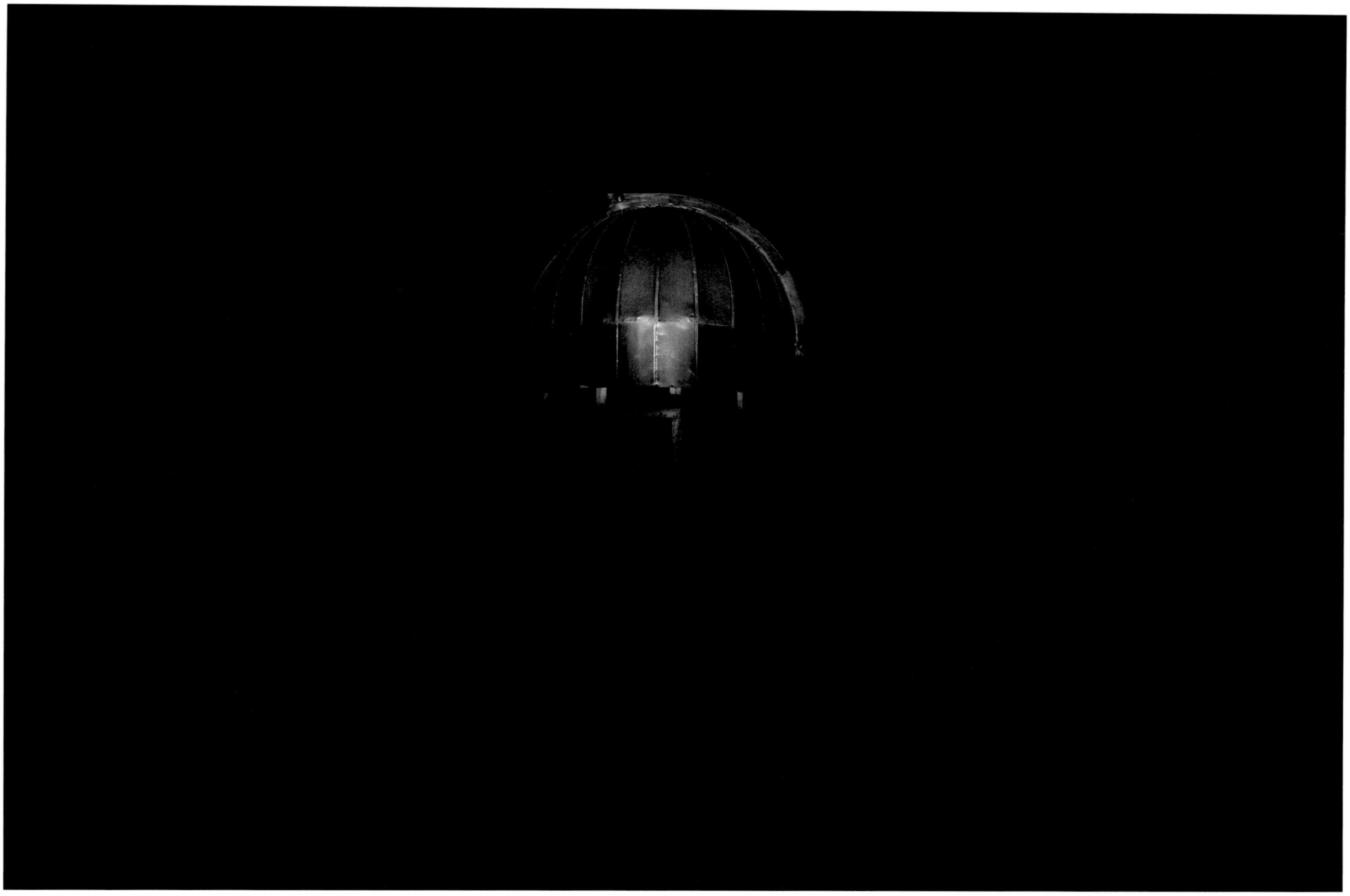

PLATES

01 L'Observatoire de Haute-Provence, France 2022

02 Nilay Mokashi, Kesariwada Jyotirvidya Observatory, Jyotirvidya Parisanstha (||ज्ञानस्य नरि्मलं नेत्रं ज्योतषि्यकमनुत्तमम्||), Pune, Maharashtra, India 2022

03 Nyrölä Observatory, Jyväskylä, Finland 2019

04 Home of Peter Anderson, Brisbane, Queensland, Australia 2022

05 L'Observatoire de Haute-Provence, France 2022

06 Painted canvas on the Astropeiler radio telescope site, Bad Münstereifel, Germany 2019

07 Olivier Garde, L'Observatoire de Haute-Provence, France 2022

08 Simon Dawes' old camera cooler box, Bexley Heath, United Kingdom 2023

09 Tony Vanmunster in his home observatory, Landen, Belgium 2019

10 Clanfield Observatory, Hampshire Astronomical Group, Clanfield, United Kingdom 2022

11 Home of Michael Mattiazzo, Swan Hill, Australia 2022

12 L'Observatoire de Haute-Provence, France 2022

13 Olivier Thizy and Olivier Garde at Olivier Garde's farm, Châbons, France 2019

14 Home observatory of Barry Adcock, Melbourne, Australia 2022

15 L'Observatoire de Haute-Provence, France 2022

16 On the Astropeiler radio telescope site, Bad Münstereifel, Germany 2019

17 Model moon, Starkenburg Observatory, Heppenheim, Germany 2019

18 BAA (British Astronomical Association) Deep Sky Meeting, Cheltenham, United Kingdom 2019

19 L'Observatoire de Haute-Provence, France 2022

20 Nyrölä Observatory, Jyväskylä, Finland 2019

21 Hankasalmi Observatory, Hankasalmi, Finland 2019

22 Arto Oksanen, Hankasalmi Observatory, Hankasalmi, Finland 2019

23 Clanfield Observatory, Hampshire Astronomical Group, Clanfield, United Kingdom 2022

24 Dave Gault in his home observatory, Blue Mountains, New South Wales, Australia 2022

25 Trevor Barry's custom telescope, Broken Hill, New South Wales, Australia 2022

26 Model observatory, Starkenburg Observatory, Heppenheim, Germany 2019

27 Route de la Belle Etoile, Revel, France 2019

28 John Broughton, Gold Coast, Queensland, Australia 2022

29 Jack Newtons observatory B&B home, Osoyoos, Canada 2019

30 Christian Buil and Valérie Desnoux, L'Observatoire de Haute-Provence, France 2022

31 Blue Mountain Observatory, Leura, New South Wales, Australia 2022

32 In the back of Chris Wyatt's 4x4, Walcha, New South Wales, Australia 2022

33 Old telescope near Northholt Branch Observatory, West London, United Kingdom 2019

34 L'Observatoire de Haute-Provence, France 2022

35 Home observatory of Olivier Thizy, Route de la Belle Etoile, Revel, France 2019

36 Nyrölä Observatory, Jyväskylä, Finland 2019

37 Martin Crow's home observatory, Burnham-on-Crouch, United Kingdom 2023

38 Rémy Chirié, L'Observatoire de Haute-Provence, France 2022

39 Kesariwada Jyotirvidya Observatory, Jyotirvidya Parisanstha (||ज्ञानस्य नरि्मलं नेत्रं ज्योतषि्यकमनुत्तमम्||), Pune, Maharashtra, India 2022

40 Olivier Garde on his farm, Châbons, France 2019

41 Home of Rod Stubbings, Tetoora Road, Victoria, Australia 2022

42 Chris Wyatt's 4x4 and custom telescope, Walcha, New South Wales, Australia 2022

43 Hankasalmi Observatory, Hankasalmi, Finland 2019

44 Nyrölä Observatory, Jyväskylä, Finland 2019

45 Kesariwada Jyotirvidya Observatory, Jyotirvidya Parisanstha (||ज्ञानस्य नरि्मलं नेत्रं ज्योतषि्यकमनुत्तमम्||), Pune, Maharashtra, India 2022

46 L'Observatoire de Haute-Provence, France 2022

47 Kesariwada Jyotirvidya Observatory, Jyotirvidya Parisanstha (||ज्ञानस्य नरि्मलं नेत्रं ज्योतषि्यकमनुत्तमम्||), Pune, Maharashtra, India 2022

48 Home of Peter Anderson, Brisbane, Queensland, Australia 2022

49 Trevor Barry's home obsercatory, Broken Hill, New South Wales, Australia 2022

50 Mark Blackford, Macksville, Australia 2022

51 Taurus Hill Observatory, Varkaus, Finland 2019

AUSTRALIA

24 DAVE GAULT, BLUE MOUNTAINS
An occultations observer, he is co-discoverer of the binary nature of the asteroid '(172376) 2002 YE25,' collaborating with fellow Australian amateur Peter Nosworthy. He also has an interest in photography—a picture by Ansel Adams sits on his wall.

25, 49 TREVOR BARRY, THE MINING TOWN OF BROKEN HILL
It was an eight-hour drive, through the bush, from Melbourne at night by moonlight to the home observatory of Trevor Barry, a former mine worker who in later life caught a second wind in his sails. Trevor is now a well-known amateur astronomer observing Saturn and is a furious contributor to professional research. His custom 408mm F4.5 Newtonian telescope is imprinted with care, attention, and NASA stickers. We sat in his office as Trevor described his recent collaborative efforts observing a cyclone at 50°N in the atmosphere of Saturn—the source of eight separate convective storms. He was enthralled by it and before long, I was too.

'Our neighbourhood, over the back fence, there's Mars, Jupiter, Saturn. They're really close by. Like that's a cut lunch and a bottle of water and you're there, sort of thing... we have to know our own backyard,' said Trevor in a broadcast interview in 2018. He later added, 'What does it make me feel? Insignificant.'

28 JOHN BROUGHTON, GOLD COAST
I was introduced to John via email whilst I was in Australia and I hastily made plans to see him. He wrote to me: 'since you're a photographer, we have a number of species of wild birds visiting every day that are tame enough to be hand fed, including cockatoos, kookaburras, butcher birds, rainbow lorikeets, myna birds, a bush turkey and a pheasant.' I was greeted by a pleasingly photogenic flurry of feathers.

A prolific former amateur Near-Earth Asteroid observer and hunter, he designed and built an automated 0.5m f/2.7 reflector from which most of his observations were derived.

He has reported tens of thousands of astrometric observations to the Minor Planet Centre between 1997 and 2008, which included 1,200 Solar System discoveries, two of which are comets. Two others are potentially dangerous asteroids.

32, 42 CHRIS WYATT, WALCHA
His telescope is another self-built affair. Chris observes comets by eye with printed star charts to hand as aid. We drove in his 4x4 to a local field and as it got dark, he pushed me to stay a little longer. Lining up the scope he beckoned me to look through it—just 'floating' there were Jupiter and the Galilean moons strung about it like pearls on a great planetary necklace.

41 ROD STUBBINGS, TETOORA ROAD, VICTORIA
In the countryside to the east of Melbourne, Rod's self-built home and home observatory look out over rolling hills. He is a variable star observer, but with a difference—Rod does it purely by eye. In fact, he claims to be only the third person in the last 100 years to have surpassed 400,000 visual variable star observations. As of April 2024 he was at 407,000.

'I remember the first time I found Mars at 3:00am one chilly morning; it looked like an orange peel.' said Rod about an early encounter with astronomy.

By day, Rod works as a plumber. 'The local builders know that if the weather's good, I won't be on site until smoko,' he said in a 2024 Science in Public article.

CANADA

29 JACK NEWTON, OSOYOOS
I drove from Spokane, Washington, US up and over the border into Canada to see him, arriving shortly after a bear wandered through his property. Jack is a prolific amateur supernova hunter who, with his wife, runs an astronomy themed B&B situated along a ridge overlooking Osoyoos. Of particular note are his efforts in search of the Progenitor of the Type Ib Supernova 2010O in Arp 299 where he claims to be the first Canadian amateur to be awarded time as an investigator on the Hubble Space Telescope. SN 2010O was a co-discovery by Jack and fellow amateur Tim Puckett. In Jack's rooftop observatory, red-lit and in hushed tones, I found him and some B&B guests discussing the likelihood of extra-terrestrial visitations to our home planet.

Jack's B&B sadly closed its doors for good in 2023.

FRANCE

1, 5, 7, 12, 15, 19, 30, 34, 38, 46 L'OBSERVATOIRE DE HAUTE-PROVENCE

The annual site of Spectro Star Party—probably the only such gathering of amateur and professional astronomers involved in spectroscopy (the study of the absorption and emission of light and other radiation by matter). I disembarked my taxi to a field littered with small telescopes, ghoulishly covered against the harsh summer sun, sat silent in anticipation of the night. As the light dimmed, amateurs and professionals worked together, side by side. Collaborations though, sometimes took a sweeter note; Christian Buil and Valérie Desnoux, who are married, sat side by side, night after night, in quiet spectroscopic observation. It takes place on the grounds of the professional, Haute-Provence Observatory, which has seen better days.

'You may not have time to do everything, because there is also a swimming pool on the site, hiking trails in the scrubland around the site, singing cicadas, some opportunity to take a nap… It will give an excuse to return the following year.' From the website of the operator, Shelyak Instruments. Shelyak is named after the second brightest star in the Lyra constellation: beta Lyrae.

After four nights, the same taxi driver who had left me there, laughing at my inability to communicate (he was as good at English as I was at French), picked me up from the observatory gate.

27, 35 ROUTE DE LA BELLE ETOILE, REVEL

'Route of the Beautiful Star' named by amateur spectroscopist Olivier Thizy, who convinced the local authorities to rename his local road the same.

Olivier gave me a lift back to the station; we left a little early on his request to catch the market on the way down where he purchased some local walnut oil for me. Not having hold baggage, I couldn't fly home with it. We agreed he would bring it the following year when I arranged to meet him at Spectro Star Party at L'Observatoire de Haute-Provence. The Covid-19 pandemic saw it pushed to the following year—he couldn't make it. I like to think my walnut oil is still waiting for me along Route de la Belle Etoile.

FINLAND

3, 20, 21, 22, 36, 43, 44, 51 HANKASALMI, TAURUS HILL AND NYRÖLÄ OBSERVATORIES

The sun had weakly peeked its head above the parapet for a short period and withdrawn as I travelled from Jyväskylä to Varkaus and subsequently back again. The three observatories that make up the Finnish PROAM Network span the girth of the country. Arto Oksanen, a member of the network and a variable star observer, drove us.

Finland can be cold, but it's the little things that one must do to operate an observatory on a budget this far north. As I looked on at dusk, Arto thawed the padlock to the Nyrölä observatory dome with hot water.

Trying to maximize the scientific output of observations, those from the network are, for example, monitoring the recurrent nova M31N 2008-12a for nova outburst—taking a deep image every clear night to check if the nova is visible. In tandem with observers around the globe, they also make observations of other high interest targets like eclipsing cataclysmic variables.

GERMANY

6, 16 BAD MÜNSTEREIFEL

Hand painted, punctured with LED's and lying in an empty room of the Astropeiler radio telescope site, I was later told this vision of the universe, depicting Barnard 68, was an artifact of educational outreach.

A professional relic from an earlier era of radio astronomy, the telescope is kept functional and relevant by a voluntary team of amateurs and professionals. They often spend time in local schools trying to engage students in all things cosmic.

17, 26 STARKENBURG OBSERVATORY, HEPPENHEIM

Wandering around with Rainer Kresken, a flight dynamics engineer at the European Space Agency, I came upon a little model of the site rendered in plastic and wood, with the kind of miniature trees one finds on model railways. Extensive for an amateur observatory, it is a shared facility making observations of near-earth objects.

INDIA

2, 39, 45, 47 KESARIWADA OBSERVATORY, PUNE, MAHARASHTRA

Jyotirvidya parisanstha (||ज्ञानस्य निर्मलं नेत्रं ज्योतिष्यकमनुत्तमम्||) founded in 1944, proclaims to be the oldest amateur astronomical society in the country. I travelled by rickshaw from the hotel to their office where I was welcomed by members. Then onwards to their observatory, sitting atop a nondescript building in the city, a little beacon of amateur science amongst the Pune skyline.

Using a 12" 1200mm scope, JVP members make variable star observations and submit them to the AAVSO (American Association of Variable Star Observers). They tend to use an 11" 3000mm for planetary imaging and also report asteroid occultation data to the IOTA (International Occultation Timing Association).

UNITED KINGDOM

10, 23 HAMPSHIRE ASTRONOMICAL GROUP, CLANFIELD

Around 100 kilometres south west of London some members of Hampshire Astronomical society are contributing photometric observations to the ExoClock program—a project to monitor the ephemerides of transiting exoplanets in the lead up to the European Space Agencies' ARIEL space telescope launch, due in 2029. The program is galvanising amateurs to get involved. The slight dip in light can sometimes be seen by a somewhat modest commercial telescope and with an appropriate camera attached, the transit can be recorded.

18 THE BRITISH ASTRONOMICAL ASSOCIATION (BAA)

'The BAA was officially formed [...] in 1890 to rival the Royal Astronomical Society (RAS). To be cheaper for members and to welcome women—which the RAS did not. Since then, BAA has encouraged amateurs to make scientifically valuable observations, often in collaboration with professional colleagues.' (*Memoirs of the British Astronomical Association*, vol. 36, pp.1-132)

Occultation: the interruption of the light from a celestial body or of the signals from a spacecraft by the intervention of a celestial body.

Nova: a star showing a sudden large increase in brightness and then slowly returning to its original state over a few months.

Minor Planet Centre: a division of the IAU, responsible for the designation of minor bodies in the solar system: minor planets; comets; and natural satellites, as well as for the collection, computation, checking and dissemination of astrometric observations and orbits for minor planets and comets.

Eclipsing cataclysmic variables: binary star systems consisting of a white dwarf primary that is accreting matter from a normal companion star.

Variable Star: a star that varies in its apparent brightness over time from the observer's perspective.

Transiting exoplanet: a planet outside our solar system that by chance temporarily transits in front of its host star, relative to the observer.

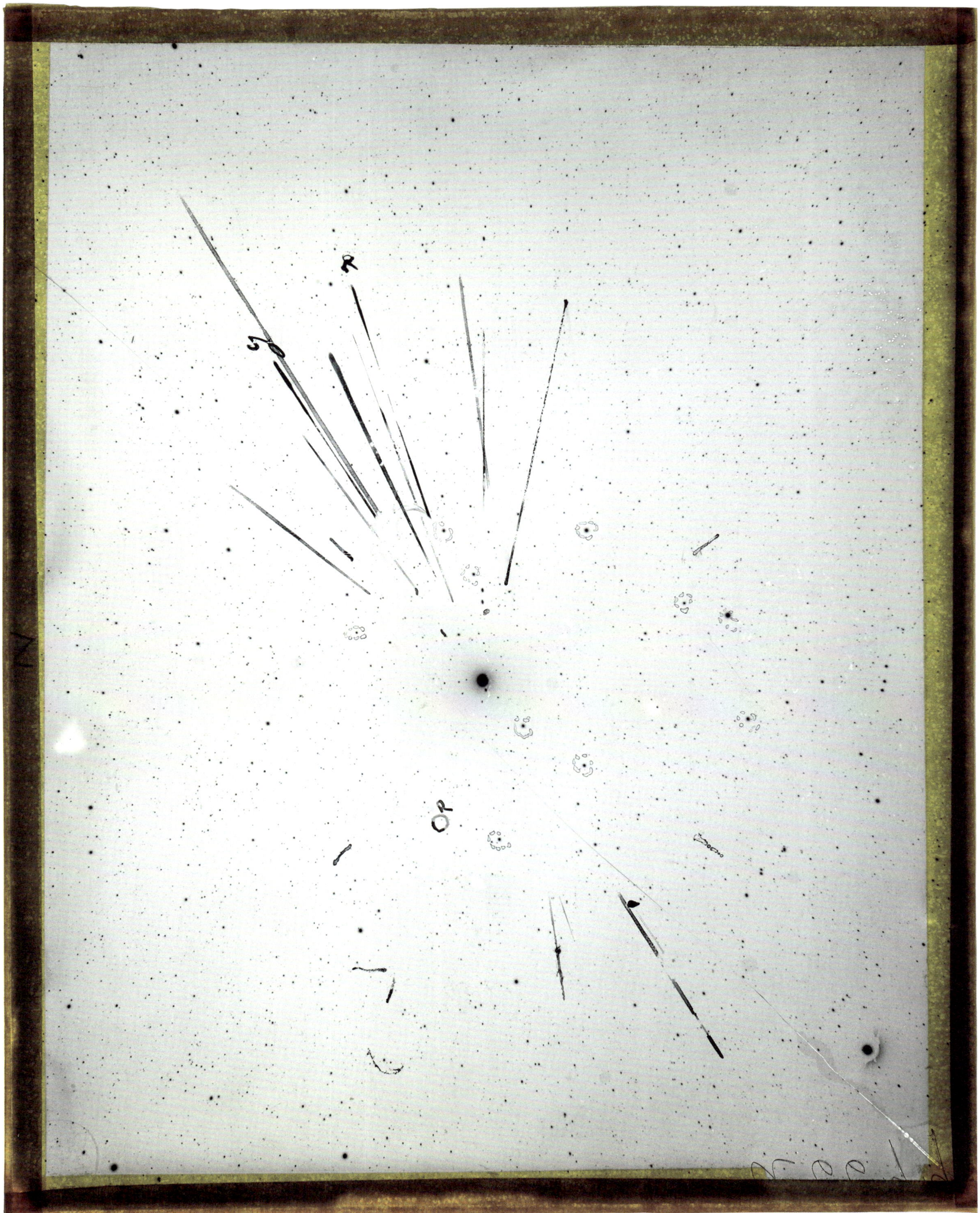

NO. a06677

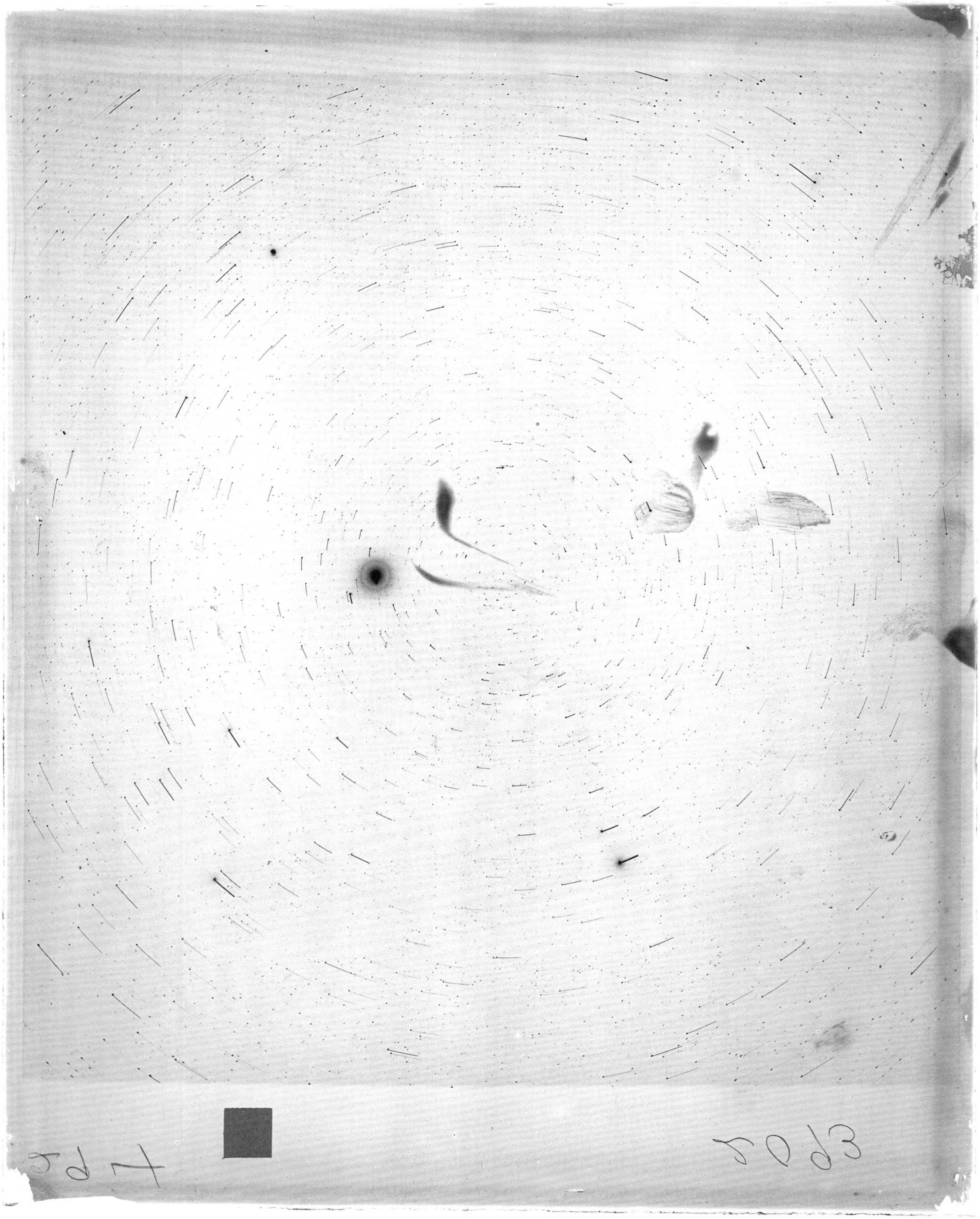

NO. b2093

NO. b02324

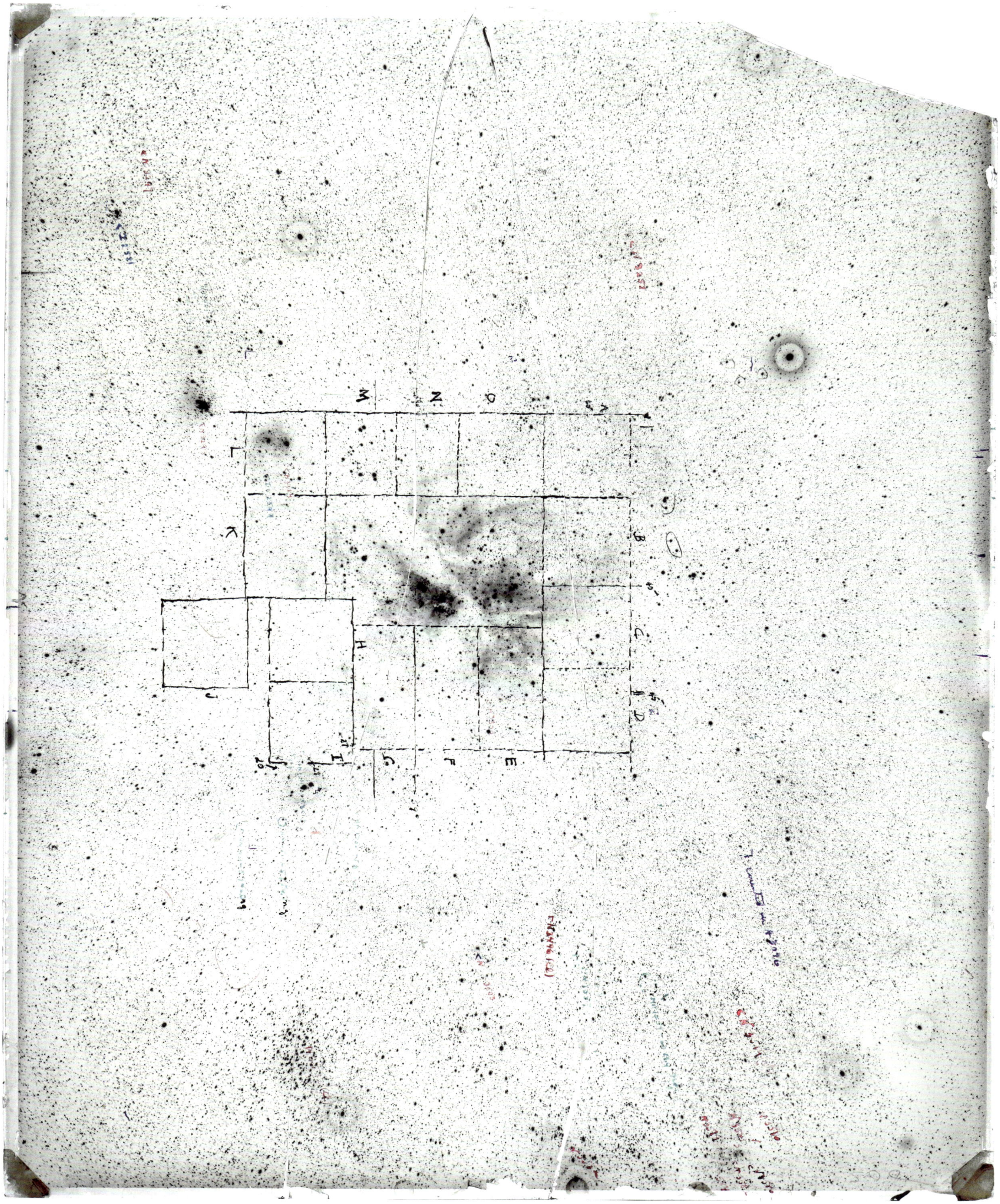

NO. a02208

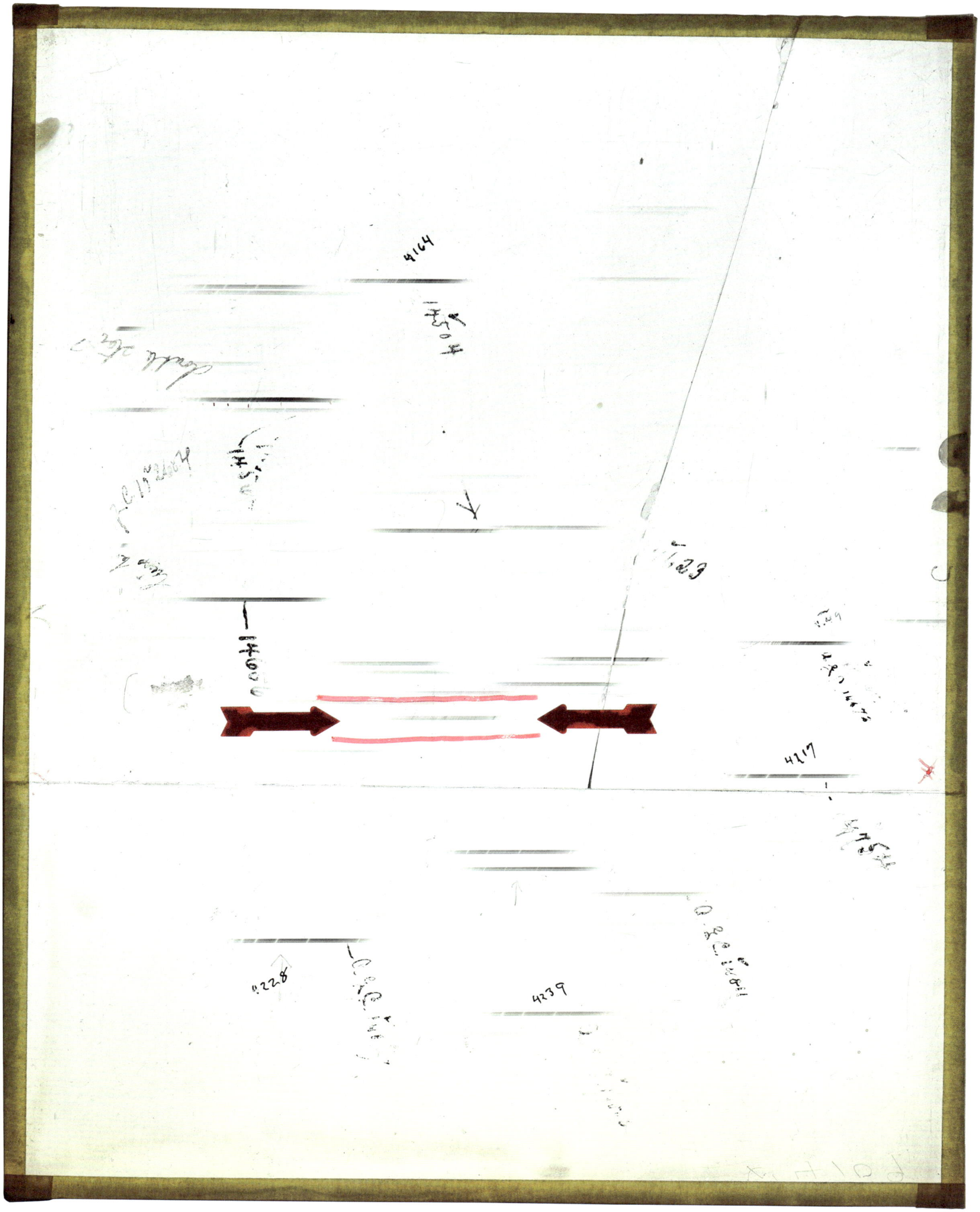

NO. x04709

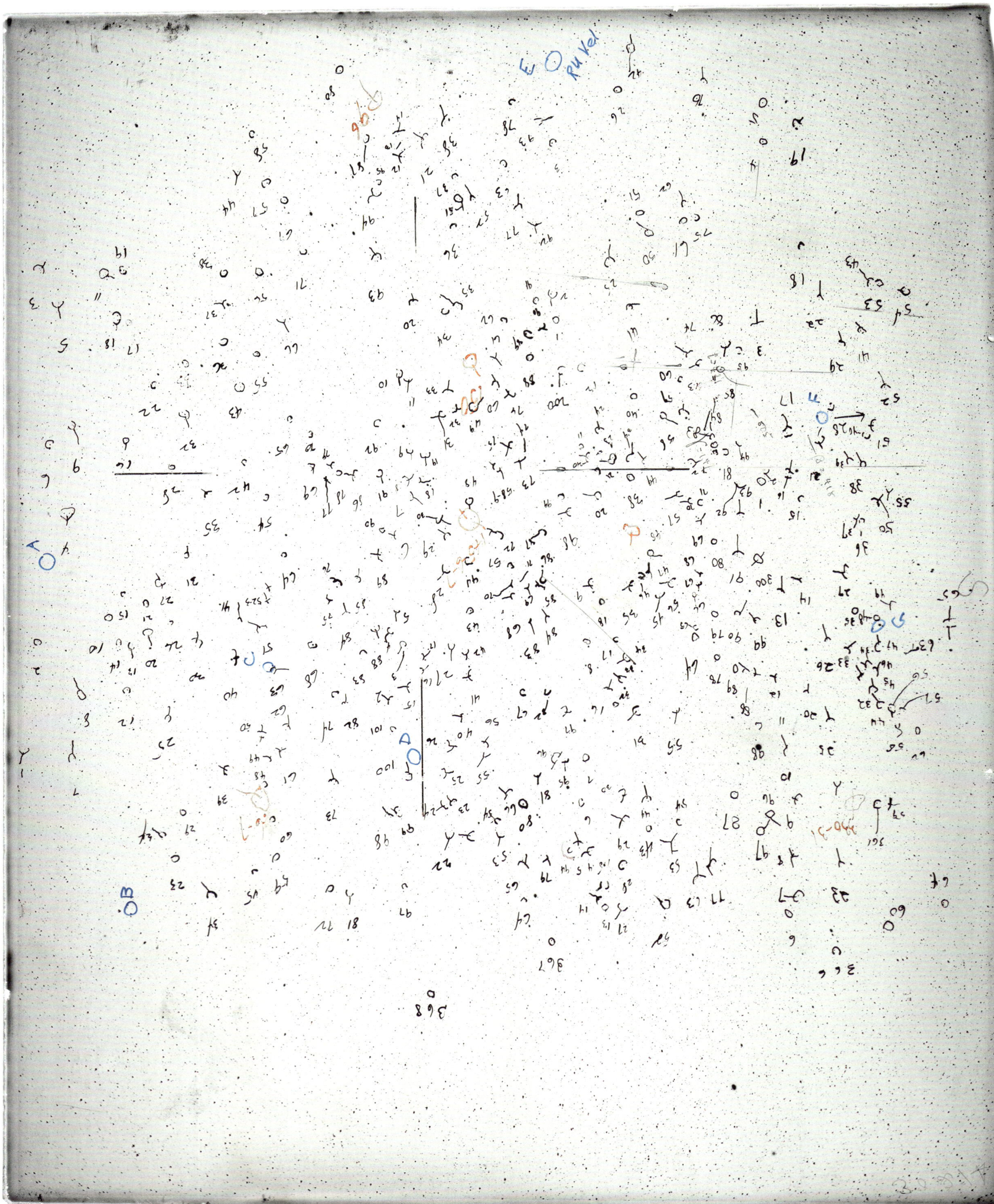

NO. a03021

NO. x07461

NO. i10321

ANDROMEDA

Examined for doubles
Partly checked - M.E.M.
using MC 27463, 27466
(MC 26157 - no good)

1900 center: 0 36.7, + 40.1

Galactic Long. 90 (89.3) Lat. -22 (-22.0)

Old nebulae - 3 N.G.C.

New nebulae - 458

Possible globular clusters - 124 (marked in green)

Examined Jan. 16, 1935 - M.C.M.

Neb. "A"

AND. NEB.

No. MC 27415

CLASS, L

R. A. $0^h 40^m$

DEC. + 40.

m 2 (double images)

QUALITY,

DATE, Sept. 10-11, 1934

EXPOSURE, 3^h

S

2, 427, 691. 702

Rej for example plate
galaxy counts
LS 2017

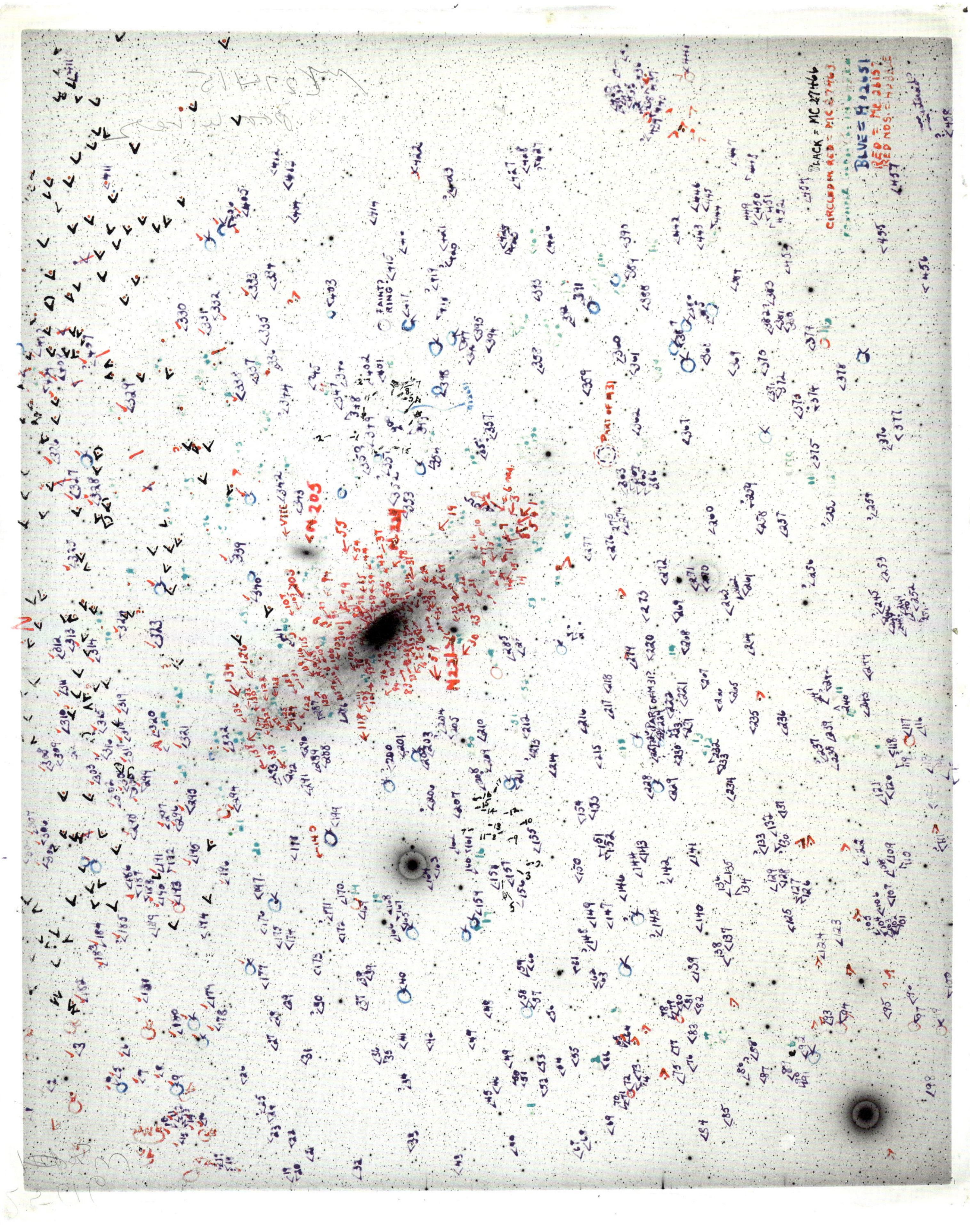

NO. mc27415

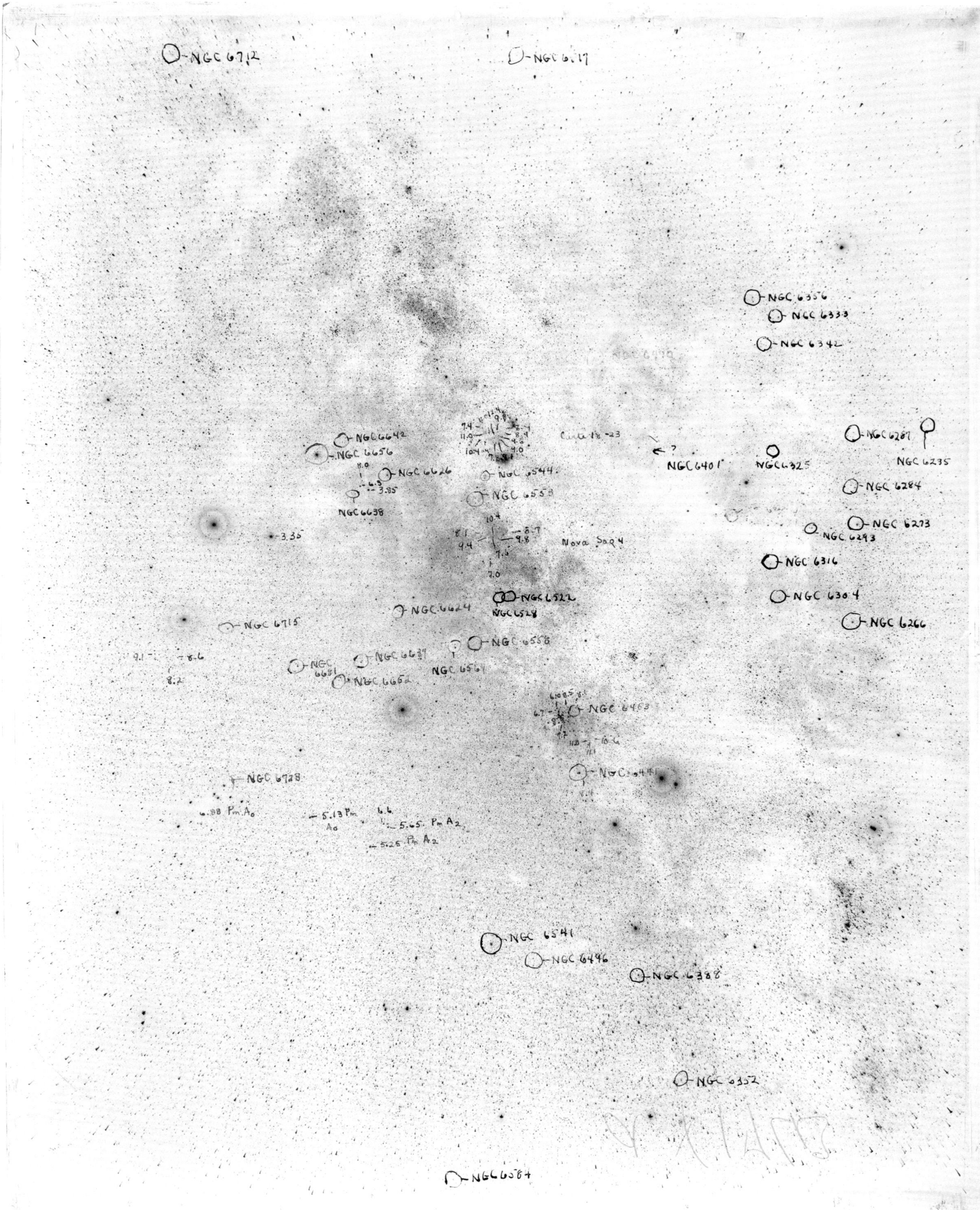

NGC 6712
NGC 6356
NGC 6333
NGC 6342
NGC 6642
NGC 6656
NGC 6626
NGC 6638
NGC 6544
NGC 6553
NGC 6401
NGC 6325
NGC 6235
NGC 6284
NGC 6273
NGC 6293
Nova Sag 4
NGC 6316
NGC 6522
NGC 6528
NGC 6304
NGC 6266
NGC 6624
NGC 6715
NGC 6558
NGC 6637
NGC 6681
NGC 6652
NGC 6569
NGC 6453
NGC 6723
NGC 6541
NGC 6496
NGC 6388
NGC 6352
NGC 6584

NO. ax1743

NO. b41215

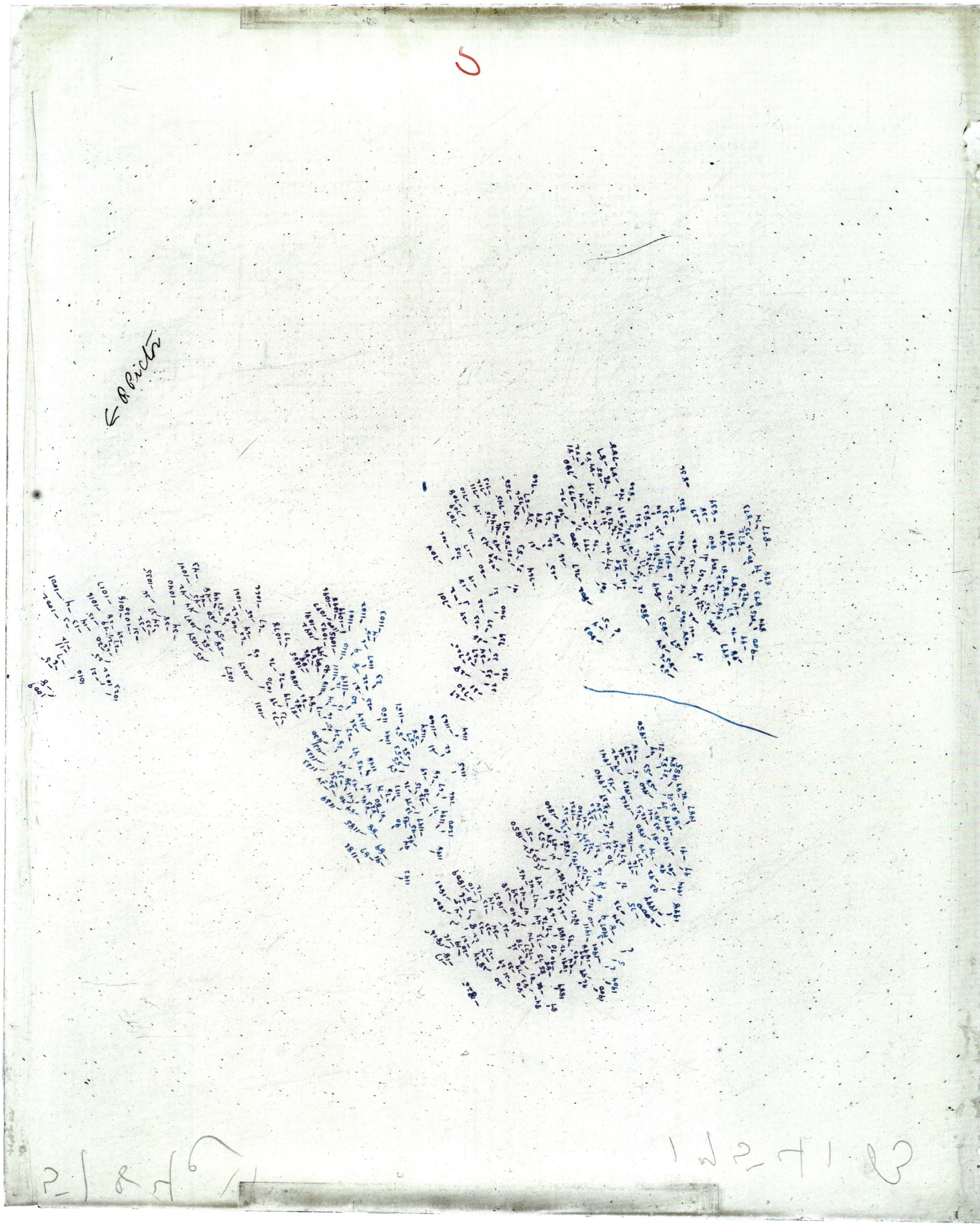

NO. b17541

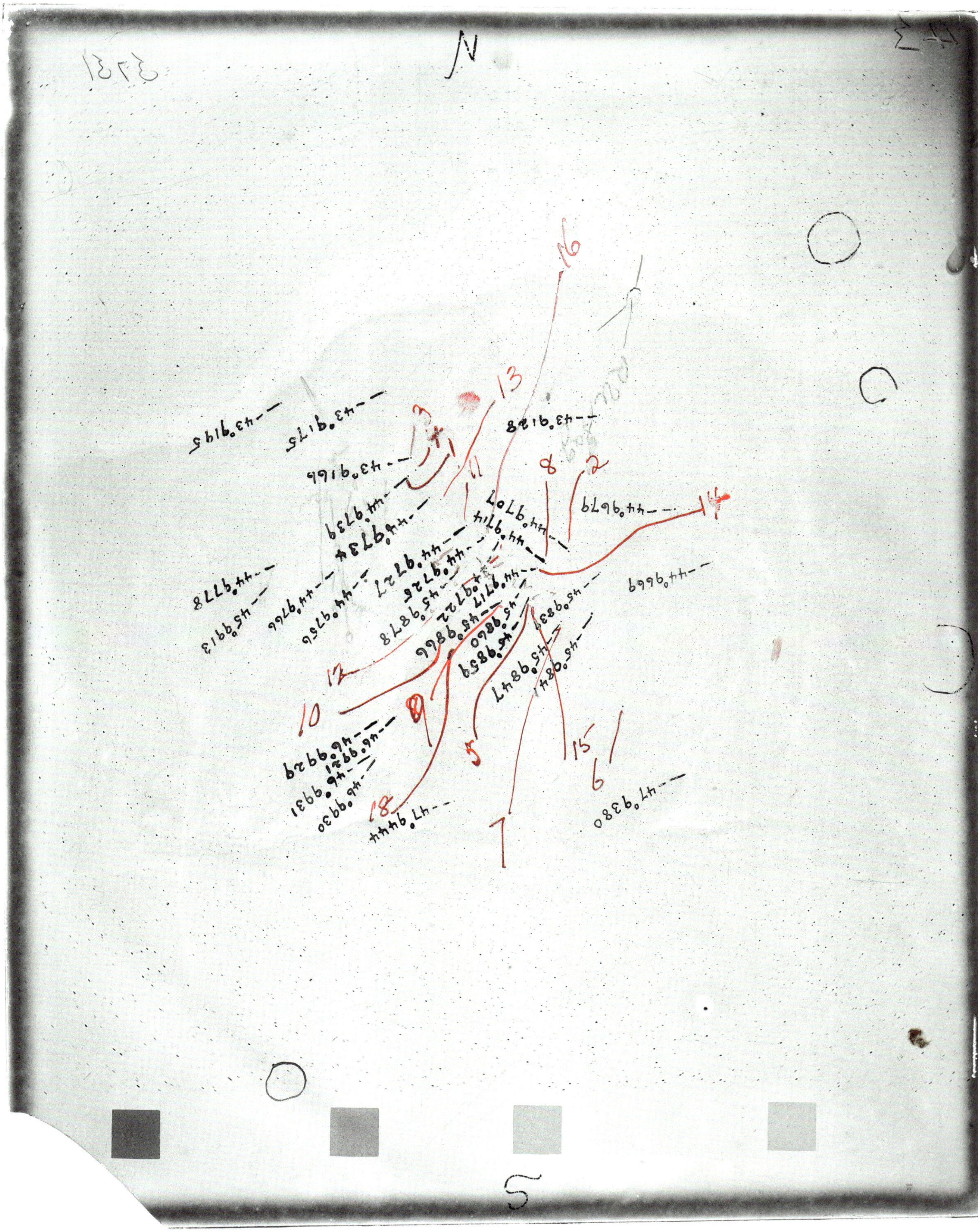

NO. b03731

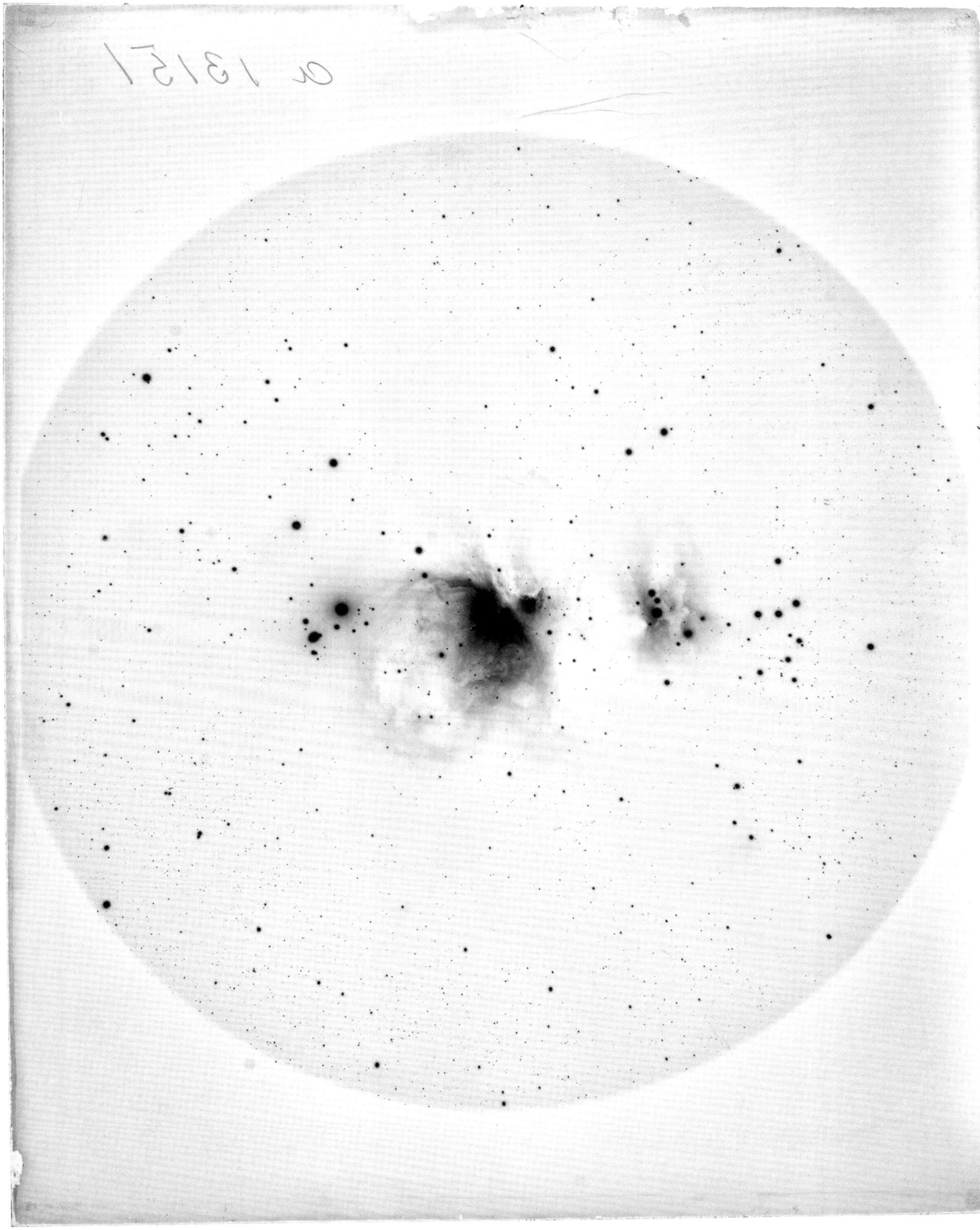

NO. a13151

NO. a06677
CLASS, Unknown
R. A. 21h 27m
DEC. -15.8°
QUALITY, 4
DATE, Apr. 19, 1904
EXPOSURE, 120 m

NO. b2093
CLASS, H
R. A. Unknown
DEC. +90°
QUALITY, 4
DATE, Dec. 22, 1887
EXPOSURE, 127 m

NO. b02324
CLASS, H
R. A. 3h 38m
DEC. +24.0°
QUALITY, Unknown
DATE, Feb. 9-10, 1888
EXPOSURE, 54 m

NO. a02208
CLASS, Unknown
R. A. 10h 40m
DEC. -59°
QUALITY, Unknown
DATE, Jan. 31, 1897
EXPOSURE, 240 m

NO. x04709
CLASS, G
R. A. 10h 41m
DEC. -59.2°
QUALITY, 5
DATE, Jun. 2, 1893
EXPOSURE, 31 m

NO. a03021
CLASS, Unknown
R. A. 11h 11m
DEC. -52.5°
QUALITY, 5
DATE, May 24, 1898
EXPOSURE, 63

NO. x07461
CLASS, P
R. A. 12h 03m
DEC. -50.2°
QUALITY, 5
DATE, Apr. 18, 1896
EXPOSURE, 59 m

NO. i10321
CLASS, L
R. A. 07h 24m
DEC. +48.4°
QUALITY, 3
DATE, Dec. 27, 1893
EXPOSURE, 10 m

NO. mc27415
CLASS, L
R. A. 0h 40m
DEC. +40°
QUALITY, Unknown
DATE, Sept. 10-11, 1934
EXPOSURE, 3 h

NO. ax1743
CLASS, L
R. A. 18h 00m
DEC. -30.0°
QUALITY, 5
DATE, Jul. 6-7, 1926
EXPOSURE, 90 m

NO. b41215
CLASS, M
R. A. 23h 42m
DEC. +7.3°
QUALITY, 4
DATE, Apr. 21-22, 1910
EXPOSURE, 30 m

NO. b17541
CLASS, L
R. A. 5h 8m
DEC. -47.6°
QUALITY, 4
DATE, Oct. 1, 1896
EXPOSURE, 10 m

NO. b03731
CLASS, H
R. A. 19h 55m
DEC. – 45.0°
QUALITY, 4
DATE, Jul. 5, 1889
EXPOSURE, 60 m

NO. a13151
CLASS, L
R. A. 5h 32m
DEC. -5.5°
QUALITY, 4
DATE, Oct. 30, 1924
EXPOSURE, 180 m

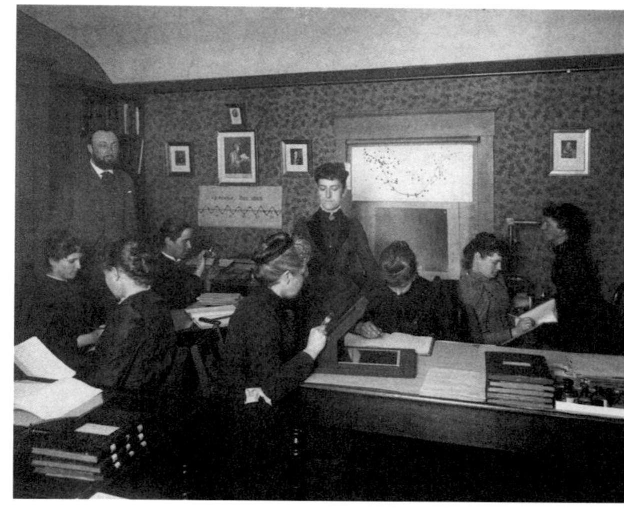

Observatory computer room and staff, 1891 (Harvard University Archives)

After the unexpected demise of amateur astronomer Henry Draper in 1882 in New York, his wife, Anna Palmer Draper, resolved to continue his work. She established The Henry Draper Memorial Fund, which played a central role in the employment of women at Harvard College Observatory. Known as 'Computers' these women measured and catalogued the stars, annotating the astronomical glass plate negatives by hand.

Many professional astronomers were once amateurs. The latter often leads to the former. But there is a gossamer thread between them, it's the subject of this book, a sort of grey zone of possibility where an amateurs' reach can exceed their grasp.

I am no astronomer, it must be said, but my interest runs deep. When I was a child, my grandfather would hoist me atop his shoulders, point upwards and name the constellations. I was too young then, to now recall much else of him. So, I have this single early image in my mind, more like a photograph than a memory.

Thank you to:

My parents, whose support through my interests (there were many) was as unrelenting as me. For the extravagance of film school, and of course, the cameras.

My wife, Natalie, without whom this book (especially the text) would have been much poorer.

Joel Fowler, for the Australian road trip.

Mark Power, for a timely nudge in the right direction.

Stu Smith and the team at GOST, for plucking me out of obscurity.

Harvard College Observatory and their Harvard Plate Stacks.

And finally, the amateur astronomers who kindly allowed me into their homes and observatories.

Further reading:

The Demon-Haunted World: Science as a Candle in the Dark by Carl Sagan (Random House, 1997)

The Glass Universe: The Hidden History of the Women Who Took the Measure of the Stars by Dava Sobal (4th Estate, 2016)

Route de La Belle Etoile
First published in 2024
by GOST Books, London

info@gostbooks.com
gostbooks.com

Captions for the Star Glass photographs were taken from a combination of plate jacket photographs, logbook data and plate information on the DASCH (Digital Access to a Sky Century at Harvard) and StarGlass web applications.

Quote (page 01) first published in *Pale Blue Dot: A Vision of the Human Future in Space* by Carl Sagan (Ballantine Books, 1997)

Edited and designed by GOST:
Rossella Castello, Katie Clifford, Gemma Gerhard, Justine Hucker, Allon Kaye, Eleanor Macnair, Claudia Paladini, Ana Rocha

Printed in Italy by EBS

British Library cataloguing-in publication data.
A catalogue record of this book is available from the British Library.

ISBN 978-1-915423-50-4

On the 14th of June 2024, I flew back from Italy where this book had just been printed. My wife and I chatted and cuddled for a short while on the sofa at home, in Ealing.

She left for an evening run and was hit by a car.

She died almost instantly.

This book, in so many ways, is a product of Natalie's support, of her love. Her fingerprints remain throughout.

it's warm and deep
you'll drown
if you don't drink
—Natalie Grover